BRIAN

BERTRAND RUSSELL AT THE FREE TRADE HALL
HEROES OF A LITERARY LONER

First published in paperback by
Michael Terence Publishing in 2024
www.mtp.agency

Copyright © 2024 Brian Darwent

Brian Darwent has asserted the right to be identified as the author of this work in accordance with the Copyright, Designs and Patents Act 1988

ISBN 9781800948945

No part of this publication may be reproduced, stored in a retrieval system, or transmitted, in any form or by any means, electronic, mechanical, photocopying, recording or otherwise, without the prior permission of the publishers

Front cover design (AI)
Michael Terence Publishing

...practicing any art - be it painting, music, dance, literature, or whatever - is not a way to make money or become famous. It's a way to make your soul grow... And what Bill Gates is saying is, "Hey, don't worry about making your soul grow. I'll sell you a new program and, instead, let your computer grow, year after year after year..."

Kurt Vonnegut
Like Shaking Hands with God

Contents

1: *THE FORMATIVE YEARS OF A LITERARY LONER* *1*
2: *BERTRAND RUSSELL AT THE FREE TRADE HALL* ... *11*
3: *WHO READS SOMERSET MAUGHAM TODAY?* *23*
4: *A CONFEDERACY OF DUNCES* *38*
5: *THE BROTHER* *42*
6: *REVIVING SAROYAN* *46*
7: *KURT VONNEGUT AT CHELTENHAM* *61*
8: *TRYING TO READ JOHN IRVING* *72*
9: *EVELYN WAUGH AND THE TWITCH UPON THE THREAD* *77*
10: *THE SAD END OF MALCOLM MUGGERIDGE* *81*
11: *SAMUEL BUTLER REVISITED* *90*
12: *JACK TREVOR STORY: AN UNAUTHORISED BIOGRAPHY* *94*
13: *HL MENCKEN AND THE GODS OF OLD* *107*
14: *THURBER v WODEHOUSE* *111*
15: *HENRY JAMES: A PERSONAL VIEW* *121*
16: *MY LIFE WITH JK GALBRAITH* *125*
17: *ISN'T FIFTY YEARS ENOUGH?* *130*

ABOUT THE AUTHOR *137*

Brian Darwent (Self Portrait)

1

THE FORMATIVE YEARS OF A LITERARY LONER

How did I get to be such a book lover - surrounding myself with them, at times almost tripping over them? And what made me turn to writing – as a very serious hobby, if not as a career, fifty years ago? It doesn't make sense. I mean, it's not as if there was a literary tradition of any kind in my family. There wasn't even that much of a *reading* tradition.

Well, my dad did read quite a lot - usually library books - although he had hardly been encouraged in that direction in his own early years. When he was a boy, my grandmother would strike a match and quietly set fire to any reading material he or his siblings dared bring to the table, always taking them by surprise. He had to read with a torch, under the bedclothes. Not that he was any kind of weakling. He and his pals used to go swimming in the local canal, having been forbidden to do so. My grandmother would react to this disobedience by following them and stealing their clothes, leaving them to dash home through the cobbled streets naked. But he continued as best he could to read, even though my mother, in their early married life, was exasperated by it. She wasn't much of a reader herself. Far too busy for that.

My dad's origins were in Derbyshire, but *his* father - looking for work, I expect - moved the family to a rough area of Warrington when he was no more than six. He remembered the green hills for the rest of his life. My mother lived in the same slum street. After they married they escaped to a pleasant suburb of the town - new, red-brick semis on a country lane, surrounded by farmland. I've never understood how they managed it, but that appeared to be the limit of their aspirations. He worked for the same company all his life, latterly in a supervisory role, wearing a brown smock. He never knew unemployment. My mum was a barmaid. Their ambition for my older brother and me was no more than that we should be respectable, and that we should find and keep a steady job. So ours could not be described as an intellectual household, in spite of my dad's visits to the library.

We *owned* very few books. Nor were they on display. They were kept in an old bedding box in their bedroom. I do remember a couple of fat picture books, however. One was called *The Story of the World in Pictures*. It contained a memorable sequence of sepia photographs of a fight to the death between a shark and an octopus. The other book was *The First World War in Pictures*, and that was even more fascinating, for hidden away inside it was a picture of a young girl with no clothes on. It had the innocent caption, "A German Girl". Time was when I could still remember the page number.

But what about school? Wasn't an interest in reading - and perhaps even writing - encouraged there? Not directly, though I do have happy memories of my primary school in the 1940s. Our teachers in those days often read aloud to the class, and sometimes in the summer a teacher I have particularly fond memories of - Mrs Ford - would take us out onto the school playing field, where we would sit around her feet on the grass under a tree. Could there be a better way to introduce children to the world of books? It was a lovely field, too, despite still having two air-raid shelters. These were landscaped into a small grassy hill, however, so that you hardly noticed the steps leading down to them. The war hadn't been over very long. We hear a great deal about the austerity of those years nowadays, but it was really a time of optimism. Hadn't we *won* the war? Now things could only start to get better.

But they didn't start to get better for me at grammar school. Things were very different there. Whatever gains I'd made towards an interest in books and writing were quickly lost. It often seems to be the case that famous writers have their fledgling talent fortuitously noticed by a kindly master who, with a few quiet, well-chosen words, points them in the right direction. And such people are always remembered later with gratitude and affection in their memoirs. Did anything remotely like that happen in my own case?

Well, towards the end of my very first term our form teacher did take me aside for a quiet word, it's true. But what he had to say wasn't exactly encouraging. "You're a long way behind the others, you know, Darwent," he whispered in my ear. It knocked me back. And yet I see that in our first exams, shortly afterwards, I came in the top ten in a class of nearly thirty. still have my school report.

Smith, the man's name was. K I Smith - or "Kisser", as we called him from the start. It was a rugby school (two old boys were currently playing for England), but soccer was starting to make inroads, and one year there was a match between the masters and older boys, in the course of which Kisser took a direct hit where it hurt most. Whether the boy who kicked the ball aimed the powerful shot deliberately, though, I never did find out. All I know for sure is that it was very effective. Kisser had to be helped, bent double, from the field.

English lessons at grammar school seemed designed to put you off books for life. They weren't presented in a remotely encouraging way. One teacher we had was blind. You might think he would therefore be somehow extra good at introducing his pupils to the joys of the written word. Not a bit of it. He had his well-worn set of Braille notes, and when we were studying a novel or a Shakespeare play did no more than use them for dictation. He hadn't the smallest gift for bringing Shakespeare's language to life. In his mind everything seemed to boil down to "tragic irony", as I recall. Not an easy concept for fourteen-year-olds.

We had to do a lot of reading aloud for him. In a class of teenage boys, with a blind teacher, there would be other - unmentionable - things going on silently around you, so it was by no means easy to concentrate. But I had a terribly monotonous reading voice, anyway. Usually we would only read for a minute or two each. One time, however, he allowed me to carry on for much longer. The novel, I believe, was *Silas Marner*, which at the time would have struck me as terribly uninspiring, I'm sure. I never seemed to like any of the books we did. But after three or four minutes of reading, I began to believe I must in fact be doing rather well, so I tried my best to put as much expression as I could into my voice.

At last our teacher stopped me in mid-sentence.

"Who *is* this reading?" he enquired.

"Darwent, sir," I answered proudly.

"It's almost *unintelligible!*"

And that wasn't my *worst* moment at grammar school. That came in a Music lesson, quite early on. I had a monotonous reading voice, but I was also lumbered with a lamentable singing voice. There was probably a connection. In fact my singing voice couldn't seriously be described as a singing voice at all. Everybody on my mother's side was the same. We couldn't hold a tune to save our lives. Nor is it a condition that attracts the slightest sympathy. It is simply funny. What's more, I had known about this affliction from an early age. Teachers, even of infants, are very quick to pounce on it. If the class are going to sing nicely together, you can't have somebody spoiling it. Such a child is simply told to keep quiet, without the smallest regard for their feelings. Someone ought to do a proper study on the subject. (I don't do studies myself.)

Well, our Music teacher was a man called Jack Stirrup. He was very keen on his subject. So keen that he wanted to start a choir, or something like that. So everybody in class had to sing a scale. Up and down. There was no getting out of it. You might protest that you couldn't sing, but Jack Stirrup said he would be the judge of that - along with the rest of the class, need I add. Nor was this sprung on us. We were told a week in advance.

There followed easily the most dreadful week of my entire school life. I couldn't sleep or eat. My thoughts were fully concentrated on my coming humiliation. I tried pretending to be ill but felt that that might only delay the ordeal.

And it turned out to be every bit as terrible as I had anticipated. Unable to believe his ears, Jack Stirrup insisted that I did several encores, a wide grin gradually spreading over his normally stern face.

He then led the class in falling about with laughter.

*

I have only a single memory of what I *wrote* at school. I expect we were usually required to write essays designed to impress an examiner, there being no call for what might be termed "free writing". But there was this one time when we *were* told to write something different.

A man with the wonderful name of Herbie Gravitt was by now our English teacher. Poor Herbie was rather weedy. I can picture him now, with his thinning frizzy hair, glasses and tweed jacket with elbow patches. He used to try to hit big, growing lads about the head if they misbehaved. They would respond by crying out in mock pain and ducking away in an exaggerated manner, as if the blows were really hurting, when in truth they were little more than fly swats. Herbie would then disappear down the corridor for a breather. Some said it was for a little weep, others that he was taking one of his pills. He was having some sort of trouble with his wife as well, it was rumoured. I used to feel a bit sorry for the poor man - until the day I'm telling you about, that is.

For Herbie was capable of the odd surprise and for homework, over the weekend, he had instructed us to write for a change about something *true* in our own lives. Nor were *we* to worry about describing it in our own words. That was the whole point. *Tell it like it is!* we'd say today, although that phrase had yet to be invented.

The rest of the class appeared to accept the assignment without a murmur, but what was I to write about in *my* uneventful life. Nothing at all came to mind. For most of my five years at grammar school, rising at six-thirty, I had a long morning paper round, which took me at least an hour. Then, after my breakfast, I had a mile to walk to catch the train to school. Saturdays were different, however. After the paper round, I ran errands for an uncle who lived alone and kept an off licence in the same rough part of town where my parents had grown up. My uncle was pretty eccentric. Today he would be quickly recognised as a rabid racist, and probably put in prison.

Could I write about my typical Saturday morning - with my uncle of course as the centrepiece? It was raw material of a sort, and I could think of nothing else. So I *did*, telling it exactly like it was. I even included a few swear words, for my uncle was very free with those. I remember how he dealt with tax demands. "Income? *What* bloody income?" he would cry, tearing up the brown envelope, contents included, and letting the pieces flutter down into a bin behind the counter. In those days "bloody" was the approximate equivalent of the "f" and "c" words today.

How did Herbie Gravitt react?

He was *appalled*. And it wasn't my choice of language or subject that upset him. They didn't seem to matter. What *really* appalled him was that I appeared to be wasting my precious time doing a paper round and running errands for relatives, when I ought to be attending to my studies. "It is beyond my *comprehension*," he told the class, standing on tip-toe to deliver his judgment.

I don't want to pretend that I had an especially unhappy time at grammar school. There were kids who suffered far more than I ever did. We travelled to school by train in closed compartments, and one poor lad had his clothes stripped off most days. He would then be held up to the window as the train crossed a bridge close to a small village. His tormentors would only let him have his clothes back when the station was almost in sight. They were quite nasty times. There was no Mrs Ford. I was even capable of indulging in the odd spot of recreational bullying myself. Nor did I begin to appreciate that attending a grammar school was quite a privilege - a once in a lifetime opportunity, no less. I stuck to my paper round and failed to apply myself.

So it's hardly surprising that when the time came (1955) I failed GCE in most subjects, including English. I had been interested in maps from an early age and could draw a rough map of the *world*, never mind the British Isles, from memory, when I was about ten. Yet now I couldn't pass the Geography exam. Nor could I manage a pass in History - although years later, when my daughters had History homework, they often sought my help - and then both proceeded to pass their GCSEs in the subject. They went on to university, too.

But the academic life wasn't for me, it seemed, back in 1955. I left school at sixteen, was lucky to find an apprenticeship as a draughtsman, and went on to earn my way to a better life by that route.

*

For four or five years after leaving school I never picked up a book. Never gave books a thought. But then, after I'd passed my driving test, I began driving into Manchester at weekends, on my own. It wasn't for any special reason - driving practice as much as anything. But wandering the streets a strange thing happened. Something deep inside drew me powerfully in the direction of the bookshops.

I'd never even looked inside a bookshop of any size before, never mind actually *entered* one. When I tried, I found it nerve-racking. Were you supposed to stay silent? Was it permissible to lift the books down from the shelves and open them? Might someone in authority step forward with a polite cough and explain that people like me weren't *allowed* in such places? That seemed quite a possibility. The best two - Sherratt & Hughes in St Ann's Square, and Wilshaw's on John Dalton Street - were especially intimidating. So nervous was I that I could only stay in them for about five minutes. I would then resume my wandering of the city streets, in a thoroughly disorientated state.

Standing in St Peter's Square was the Library, but I never gave much thought to exploring that. It was a big place, and I was sure I would have to make enquiries about how to join, and where to look once I *had* joined. I didn't fancy all that. Using a library struck me, anyway, as too much like an extension of my schooldays, and in so far as I had any notion of what I was supposed to be doing, that didn't seem to be the idea at all. It would have been closed when I was in town, though, in any case.

But from the library steps, across the square, I must one day have noticed *Percival's* bookshop, standing on a corner. It looked smaller and more friendly, and when I tried going in, I felt immediately at home. They specialised in paperbacks, though good quality ones. Garish covers, with embossed gold lettering, hadn't really caught on yet. Hardback books had seemed to predominate in the two big bookshops - far too pricey for me. Now I was amongst books that I could consider buying and taking home to keep. That already seemed important to me. I little realised it, but browsing in Percival's, beginning to discover writers for myself, I was starting my literary education afresh - in my own way, on my own terms. Nor was it very long before - at great expense and almost in self-disbelief - 1 bought a brand new Imperial Good Companion typewriter, and began my own writing life.

Fifty years later, I'm still at it.

*

But why write *this* book?

Well, firstly in an attempt to show that books - *real* books - and their authors can have a deep and lasting meaning in one's life, in an age now facing the complete domination of communication, entertainment, and heaven knows what else, by electronic gadgetry. But also because, at my age, I hate to see writers who have meant a lot to me elbowed from the shelves by new names. Of course, you can't really complain. It's the kind of thing that must happen to most people, if they live long enough. You're left with a feeling that you've been caught out somehow. Left up a blind alley. Protesting in vain.

2
BERTRAND RUSSELL AT THE FREE TRADE HALL

I wasn't just a geeky book reader and novice writer fifty years ago. I had mates, spent a lot of time in pubs, went to dances, picked up girls, went to work, did my job, earned the money I needed, fitted in well enough. But I must have been a *bit* of a loner in the more general sense, besides ploughing my own literary furrow. Something important at any rate was plainly missing from my life. How else to explain that, as a young man in my early twenties, I decided to spend what promised to be an exciting evening attending a talk by the philosopher Bertrand Russell, to be given in Manchester's famous old Free Trade Hall in the spring of 1964? I mean, the Beatles were just emerging, and the Swinging Sixties getting into their stride, yet I seemed to be at least as interested in writers and intellectuals, *some* of them ancient.

And Bertrand Russell really *was* ancient. If he were alive today, he would be close to a hundred-and-forty. His grandfather, Lord John Russell, a Whig prime minister whom he remembered well, had visited Napoleon on Elba. How very long ago that was! But Bertrand Russell also happened to be in the news in the early '60s because of his strong views on nuclear weapons and his connection with the recently formed Campaign for Nuclear Disarmament. He had quite a student following. And wasn't I a student of sorts myself?

Nevertheless, it had taken a little while before I stumbled upon the Unwin series of Russell paperbacks in Percival's. There were so many writers waiting to be discovered. I dare say I picked them up and put them down again a few times, for they were relatively expensive, though the price did vary with the thickness of the book. What did I know about philosophy? I probably asked myself. I had little idea of what the word even *meant*, at least in any technical sense. But fortunately, he wrote on more accessible subjects as well, and so at length I must have started to flick through the pages of one or two of them to see what the man had to say on such subjects as sex, religion, politics and happiness.

And I was hooked! He quickly became my great hero: intellectual, literary and moral.

*

Born in 1872, Bertrand Russell made his early academic reputation in the arcane field of mathematical logic, and had it not been for the First World War it is doubtful if I or many other people would ever have heard of him. A fierce opponent of the mindless killing - he went to prison for his activities and beliefs, though as the grandson of a prime minister and the brother of an earl (a title he would later inherit) he had an easy time - he emerged from the war a radically different creature. He would become the great philosopher-rebel of his age, a latter-day Voltaire, who championed such progressive causes as women's suffrage, birth control, socialism, liberal educational methods and religious agnosticism, through to his late but passionate campaign against nuclear weapons. The threat of nuclear war was *the* big issue in the early 1960s. We lived constantly under the threat of nuclear annihilation. Political protest was in the air. Russell was the first president of CND, and was imprisoned for the second time in his life following a sit-down demonstration by the more militant, breakaway Committee of I 00 in 1961.

A year later, he was back on the front pages as an intermediary (by letter) in the Cuban Missile Crisis, when the world really did look disaster in the face. In his book on the subject, *Unarmed Victory,* he took Kruschev's side against Kennedy, simply because he was the one who had the good sense to back down. Nevertheless, after the president's assassination, he gave his support to the "Who Killed Kennedy" committee.

He was almost ninety-two when I attended the lecture, but still near the peak of his fame and influence - remarkable in someone so old. But then his fame and reputation had grown steadily since the end of World War 1, when he would have been forty-six. His monumental *A History* of *Western Philosophy* was published when he was in his early seventies. The Nobel Prize for Literature came when he was close to eighty. The Russell-Einstein Declaration - signed by leading scientists and thinkers of the day opposed to nuclear weapons - at eighty-three. And his robust health had marched in step.

He was some kind of phenomenon. *Private Eye* joked about it, in a cartoon with the caption: "Bertrand Russell Swims Atlantic!" - showing him breasting the waves. Years earlier, though already well into his seventies, he was in a flying boat accident on a trip to Norway. Asked to comment on surviving not only the crash but a long period in icy cold water, he put it down to being a pipe smoker (a lifelong habit). This meant that he had been told to sit in a part of the plane that happened to be least affected when it crashed.

And so now, in 1964, his vigorous campaign against the American military adventure in Vietnam still lay in the future. I certainly admired his political work and the moral stances he took, and indeed his energy and stamina, but I also loved his writing style - in his more popular, though still erudite, books, through which he promoted his many causes -for its own sake. No one before or since has matched Russell's extraordinary blend of wit, lucidity, passion and humanity.

*

I was working in Manchester at the time, travelling by train from my home in Warrington into the old Central Station (now the G-Mex Centre), where I kept a bike in the left-luggage office for the last couple of miles. Such daily train journeys can be invaluable if you're embarking on something like a process of self-education, in an attempt to remedy the negative effects of schooling. Thanks to the new Routledge editions of his works, Bertrand Russell remains much in evidence in the Philosophy section in Waterstone's, the Manchester Deansgate branch (my favourite bookshop these days) at any rate, though his books are not so universally available as they were fifty years ago. On the train each day I was devouring such titles as *Why I am not a Christian*, *Marriage and Morals*, *Sceptical Essays*, *In Praise of Idleness*, *Unpopular Essays* and *The Conquest of Happiness*. They had all been around for years, even then, but had lost none of their sparkle.

But perhaps this sudden discovery of Bertrand Russell needs a little more explanation. You might well ask - since I was from a working-class background - if there weren't more suitable writers for me to seize upon? Russell was a philosopher *and* an aristocrat, which was hardly my territory. So why wasn't I put off? Why didn't I choose a writer I could more easily relate to - like DH Lawrence? I was trying to write myself. Wasn't *he* the right kind of role model for me?

Well, Lawrence and Russell had clashed during the First World War, I soon discovered (in Russell's *Portraits from Memory*). Whose side should I have taken, reading about it long afterwards?

The two were brought together by Lady Ottoline Morrell, a society hostess for arty people, who admired them both and thought they were sure to admire one another. Russell introduced Lawrence to friends at Cambridge (he was a Fellow of Trinity College), like the economist John Maynard Keynes. His new friend declared that these people were *"Dead! Dead! Dead!"*

Nevertheless, Russell was surprisingly slow to understand that he and Lawrence differed from one another more profoundly than either differed from the *Kaiser* himself. At first he had thought the novelist must possess a deeper insight into human nature than he himself enjoyed. Lawrence's emotional power in fact brought him almost to the brink of suicide, before a healthier reaction set in. In *Portraits* from *Memory*, he would later write that Lawrence's blood theories led straight to Auschwitz.

But *here* was a writer for me to admire, surely - a brave new voice sweeping aside the old if ever there was one! Yet strangely, I sided with Russell. I had read recently, too, an influential new novel - John Braine's Room *at the Top* - and seen the film of John Osborne's groundbreaking play *Look Back in Anger,* with Richard Burton. Here were newer angry voices, sweeping aside the old. But I hadn't much cared for either. So why wasn't I able to enjoy the spectacle of these brash young men from a background I was more familiar with, "storming the ramparts" (or some such phrase) of a world that had been denied to their class?

Well, to begin with, I had no real *awareness* of class. Nobody had explained it to me, so I didn't realise it was supposed to restrict your field of interests. But I may nevertheless have sensed that these people were up to no good - or at any rate no *general* good. Their concern seemed to be for themselves, not the people they grew up with. In fact they often appeared to despise their own kind.

And hadn't I seen something not so very different going on at office and factory-floor level? How did that old parody of "The Red Flag" go? *The working class can kiss my arse, I've got the foreman's job at last!* So Lawrence, the prototype for these literary social climbers, never greatly appealed to me. Bertrand Russell, by contrast, seemed to be *trying* to do genuine good in the world, rather than simply posturing. And he was miraculously still at it, still making the news, while Lawrence's tragic early death meant that he had long ago become chiefly a topic in Eng-Lit studies.

*

I had a meal in town on the evening of the talk, and then at seven-thirty joined the sizeable crowd of either genuinely interested or simply curious people waiting to enter the hall - now sadly turned into a hotel, although the frontage has been preserved. I had often been there before, though that was to see concerts by such entertainers as Ella Fitzgerald and Tony Bennett. I had never before attended anything like a public lecture, and was certainly looking forward to it. I knew no one, however, and so had to keep my excitement in check. Nowadays, I tend to believe that writers ought to resist trying to be stage performers. In 1964, I could believe that to see and hear Bertrand Russell in the flesh was sure to be a wonderfully thrilling experience.

Dressed in his usual three-piece, pin-striped grey suit, he came onto the stage in surprisingly sprightly fashion. His abundant white hair, of which it seems he was very vain (I later read that he had once found himself in competition with the architect Frank Lloyd Wright at a gathering in the Portmeirion Hotel), shone under the bright lights as he took his place and began chatting to others on the platform. Then his controversial young American secretary, Ralph Schoenman, gave him a prolonged eulogistic introduction. And at last the great man himself stepped briskly up to the microphone…

And I waited… and listened…

And… oh dear…

Nothing in the proceedings so far had prepared me for the great difficulty he would have delivering his speech…

Aside from the weirdness of his accent - he'd been born in another age, of course, into an ancient, aristocratic family - his voice was by this time high-pitched, weak and broken. He seemed to be handicapped, too, by a bad cold, and kept fumbling with a handkerchief for much of the time. NHS-style glasses perched on the end of his nose. He read the speech from notes, held close to his face, only rarely departing from the script. I can recall nothing of its content, beyond the simple fact that it was on the general theme of world peace. The audience listened in respectful silence, clapping politely, still sitting, at the end. It had lasted for about twenty minutes. It seemed longer.

Should I describe the experience as a let down? My excitement had certainly drained away long before the end, it's true. I realised how foolish I'd been to expect the man in very advanced old age to live up physically to the one 1 knew so well from his robust writings. But there was more to the event than that. Simply to be in the presence of this towering intellect - however enfeebled now, and however remote in appearance and manner from the circumstances of the 1960s - was peculiarly moving. Like being addressed, through an imperfect medium, by an enlightened being from another planet.

That, however, is an impression I probably came to later. It's more likely that I had something else on my mind as I joined the

17

people leaving the hall. I had picked up and scanned the handouts left on the seats, and may well have been asking myself if I, a poorly-paid draughtsman, could seriously contemplate taking the step of giving financial support to the organisation the event had been arranged to promote: the newly formed Bertrand Russell Peace Foundation. Did I in fact truly *believe* in the cause of world peace, in which case a sum of a hundred pounds a year might be about right? Or should I take the coward's way out and settle for ten?

I *had* joined CND, some time before, though I wasn't cut out to be an activist. I grew up near the huge American airbase at Burtonwood, which was still semi-operational in the early '60s. Also, there was a vast warehouse complex, the contents of which were a mystery. Nuclear weapons might even be stored there, it was suspected. Well, one day I heard there was to be a demonstration march, from Warrington town centre out to the base. The people I'd encountered in connection with CND struck me as pretty ineffectual, but for this important demonstration a more experienced man had been brought in. He lined us all up, with a few hand-written placards, then he endeavoured to get the chanting going.

"Yankee bases, *OUT!*" he shouted, raising a fist. "Yankee bases, *OUT! OUT! OUT!*" I'm sorry to report that my career as a political activist ended right there. I thought I would prefer a nuclear attack.

So, leaving the hall, I settled on the lower figure. Ten pounds was more than half a week's wages, but it seemed a measly contribution to funds, even so. I was very surprised, therefore, when soon afterwards I received a letter of thanks, actually signed by Bertrand Russell himself (I had seen his rather shaky signature elsewhere). I wasn't tempted to show it to anybody, though. I felt embarrassed about it, somehow, and stuffed the envelope at the back of a drawer. There it must have stayed till my father had the house cleared some years later. I was married with a growing family by then, and thinking about other things.

*

Nowadays Bertrand Russell is remembered with reverence (he died in 1970, aged ninety-seven) by older left-wing people, although otherwise he is a slightly discredited figure, I rather fear. Certainly, a TV programme in the *Reputations* series some years ago can't have helped. Nor can Ray Monk's two-volume biography (the first volume of which was reviewed in the *Guardian* by AC Grayling under the title "A Bitting for Bertie!"). His early philosophical work, important in its day, was apparently undermined by his one-time protege Wittgenstein. The social causes he fought for have largely come to pass, though the world is not yet quite the happy place he anticipated. One significant blot that has come to light is his strange advocacy, in the late 1940s, of a pre-emptive strike - or a *threatened* one - as a means of discouraging the Soviet Union from acquiring nuclear weapons.

Nor were his personal dealings always admirable. He was married four times and only his final marriage, in his eighties - living in those years in a house on the edge of the Portmeirion estate in North Wales - seems to have been really successful. Otherwise, the women in his life had a tendency to turn later into recluses. This was particularly true of his third, much younger wife, whom he married in his sixties. She was the mother of Conrad Russell, prominent in more recent times as a Liberal-Democrat peer.

Saddest of all, though, was what happened to his first wife, Alys, a Quaker (and the sister of the writer Logan Pearsall Smith), whom he left just before the First World War to take up with Ottoline Morrell. The story is told in a series of late letters Russell received from her, in the final volume of his *Autobiography*. (This was around 1949/50.) Although Alys had continued to live quite a full life (she was by now eighty), and had retained important friends, she had never got over his leaving her. She had quietly followed his progress, and for many years used to sit at the back of lecture halls, or even loiter outside his home to watch him with his children. They did meet again, all those years later, and she made an attempt to find a way back into his life even at that late stage. Sadly, it was unsuccessful. She died shortly afterwards (in 1951). Russell does little more than allow her letters to speak for themselves.

According to Ray Monk, he had a great fear of madness. There had been fears of madness in his family at the time of his marriage to Alys, but their marriage was childless. The children she later observed - a son and daughter - were with his second wife, Dora Black. And their son John *did* have problems, which weren't helped by the fact that Russell believed at the time in a psychologist's theory to the effect that boys should never be shown excessive kindness, but should be made to stand emotionally on their own feet. Nor did his attendance at the experimental school Russell and Dora had established - Beacon Hill - with its "anything goes" regime, help the boy's condition.

John went on to marry and to have children himself, but to Russell's great distress he continued to be a significant worry. In the end he more or less disowned him, insisting that the grandchildren come to live with him in North Wales. Among them was his unbalanced granddaughter, Lucy, who rather doted on him. Monk concludes his book by describing how, in tragic circumstances, Lucy burnt herself to death - in emulation of the Buddhist monks of Vietnam, it seems.

*

But then which famous person's family life isn't a mess if everything is dug up and exposed to public view? It's one of the consequences of fame. Does it mean that we must never again listen to their music, or look at their paintings, or read their written works? And Russell's more popular books can still be read with great pleasure. For those of a sceptical cast of mind they remain a delight.

Of particular pleasure for me has been a two-volume collection of short essays, *Mortals and Others*, which were first printed in the *New York American* and other Hearst newspapers during the Depression and only published in book form long afterwards. As most delightful of all, though, I would recommend a long piece from his Second World War years in America - when he fell foul of conventional opinion for a time over an academic appointment and suffered an employment boycott - entitled "An Outline of Intellectual Rubbish". It was reprinted in *Unpopular Essays*, and then later included in *The Basic Writings of Bertrand Russell*. Here's an extract:

> *…St Thomas Aquinas, the official philosopher of the Catholic Church, discussed lengthily and seriously* a *very grave problem which, I fear, modern theologians unduly neglect. He imagines a cannibal who has never eaten anything but human flesh, and whose father and mother before him had like propensities. Every particle of his body belongs rightfully to someone else. We cannot suppose that those who have been eaten by cannibals are to go short through all eternity. But, if not, what is left for the cannibal? How is he to be properly roasted in hell if all*

his body is returned to its original owners? This is a puzzling question, as the Saint rightly perceives.

*

Bertrand Russell grew up at Pembroke Lodge, on the edge of Richmond Park, the home (given to him by Queen Victoria) of his grandfather Lord John Russell. This followed the tragic early deaths of both his mother and father. They were political radicals and friends of John Stuart Mill. He had no memory of them. It was a lonely childhood, in a house of adults - his brother Frank was much older than him - though his relationship with his grandmother was a lasting influence. *Thou shalt not follow* a *multitude to do evil!,* she inscribed in a bible she gave him.

In 2007 I at last got around to visiting the house, only ever having seen it in an old painting - an illustration in Russell's *Autobiography*. From this I expected it by now to be neglected and forgotten, never having been very impressive to begin with.

The reality was very different. It has nowadays been put to modern use - banqueting suites and a cafeteria - but it's still a fascinating place to visit, all the same. The extensive wooded gardens - in which Russell would have wandered as a solitary child in the 1870s, picking up a knowledge of flowers which would stay with him throughout his life - are a delight, and the view across the river towards Windsor from the terrace, spectacular.

It was once a hunting lodge, used by Henry VIII. In no condition by then to hunt properly, the king is said to have had the deer walked in front of him, and to have fired his arrows at them from a seated position. There is also a spot in the gardens from which, according to legend, he watched for a signal that Anne Boleyn had been executed.

3
WHO READS SOMERSET MAUGHAM TODAY?

A question I'm sure only a literary *anorak* would ask is whether Bertrand Russell and Somerset Maugham ever met. It would seem strange if they didn't, for they were close contemporaries who were at the summit of their respective professions, yet I've never heard of such a meeting. Nor does Russell mention Maugham in his autobiographical writings, though Maugham certainly wrote of Russell's influence on his own views as an amateur philosopher in his autobiographical *The Summing Up*.

He also mentions him in a chapter of his 1920s travel book, *On A Chinese Screen*, in which he encounters a fellow named Henderson, a headstrong and outspoken young businessman abroad with aggressive socialist opinions. This man had at first been appalled by the treatment of the Chinese by the English, and especially by their use of the rickshaw, but in the heat of Shanghai he had gradually begun to behave more like an imperialist. He hadn't lost his hunger for books, however, in particular books by Bertrand Russell, despite having to wait months for them after they came out in England. One day, in his impatience to reach a certain bookshop to a pick up a copy of Russell's latest work (Roads *to* Freedom), he is seen giving his sweating rickshaw boy a smart kick on the bottom to hasten him along. Maugham was a humane man back there in the days of Empire, though evidently with little time for socialist theory.

Despite Russell's Nobel Prize, at the height of their respective fame Somerset Maugham was surely the more famous. So famous that he was even mentioned in a joke that did the rounds in my boyhood days. He was giving a lecture on the short story. A good one, he explained, must contain four ingredients: religion, society, sex and mystery. When asked for an example, he offered: "My God!" cried the duchess, "I'm pregnant! Who dunnit?"

We kids of the 1940s were more used to jokes about an Englishman an Irishman and a Scotsman. But the remarkable thing here isn't the joke (and there may have been some truth in it). It's the fact that working-class boys in those far-off days knew who Somerset Maugham was and that he wrote short stories. He may well have been the best-known writer on the planet. with only George Bernard Shaw and Ernest Hemingway as serious rivals. He was just about everyone's idea of a celebrated author.

Well, his books are still available today, in handsome new Vintage editions, and one or two at least (Of *Human Bondage* being the most likely) can usually be seen on the shelves in any branch of Waterstone's. But you don't get the feeling that he is much read any longer. I have never seen anybody so much as *glance* at one. Nor are his books filmed or his plays staged as often as they once were. Back in Edwardian times he'd had four plays running simultaneously in London. It caused *Punch* to publish a cartoon showing the worried ghost of William Shakespeare surveying the billboards.

His spy book, *Ashenden,* based on his First World War experiences, was made into a TV series in the early '90s, but as I recall it went largely unnoticed. Quite recently his 1920s novel *The Painted Veil,* set in China, has been filmed, with good reviews, though it appeared not to make a huge impact at the box office. I missed *The Painted Veil* at the cinema, but I did catch the film of his novella, *Up at the Villa,* ten years or so ago on television, and if I have the impression that it had a similar box-office reception, the film did make me curious to read him again after a long period. I still had his books - have I ever in my life thrown a single book away? So I dug out my old copy and reread it.

His prose now struck me as a touch archaic, and the characters in *Up at the Villa* - set in Florence - were mostly well-to-do, which isn't my preferred territory. But the theme of the story was unusual. An attractive young woman decides on a whim to give herself to a penniless student, out of kindness, with unexpected and painful consequences. And if the pace at first seemed a bit slow - Maugham, I remembered, had a way of deceiving his readers into believing that not much was going to happen in his stories - the action when it came was satisfyingly dramatic.

But regarding his prose style, there is a further slight connection with Bertrand Russell. Both were friends of a man called Eddie - or Sir Edward, as he later became - Marsh, who had a Cambridge background. Marsh and Russell had drifted far apart politically after their undergraduate days, but in Maugham's case the man was more than a friend, for according to a note at the front of an obscure wartime book, *Strictly Personal* (a copy of which I have only recently managed to pick up), he reveals that, until that particular volume, Marsh had corrected the proofs of all of his books for many years past.

This intrigued me. Maugham was fond of saying, in his essays and autobiographical writings, that English was a very difficult language. This difficulty may have had something to do with the fact that he was born in France and his first language was French. Nevertheless, he spoke and wrote English for so long that it is hard to imagine him seriously struggling with it.

And yet Marsh did not simply give the manuscripts he was handed a casual glance. Guided by *Fowler* and other authorities, he appears to have been a stickler for correct grammar, almost to the point of being a bully, and did a very conscientious job. But *Strictly Personal* (it tells of Maugham's efforts in the very early stages of the Second World War to alert the authorities in England to the true situation in France, and his subsequent escape from his home on the Riviera, in primitive conditions aboard a grimy collier, following the country's collapse) doesn't suffer much from the absence of Marsh's expert grammatical attention, I would say. Indeed, if the semicolon count is any guide, there is a distinct gain. How a writer is supposed to develop a style of his own whilst at the same time sticking rigidly to the rules laid down in *Fowler's Dictionary* of *English Usage*, I'm not at all sure.

*

But how on earth did I latch on to Somerset Maugham - another curious role model, surely? Well, predictably enough, amongst my first discoveries in Percival's bookshop, back in those early '60s days, was J D Salinger's *The Catcher in the Rye*, then only about ten years old. And for a time, like so many others, I went around seeing the rest of the human race as *phonies*. But it was Holden Caulfield who pointed me in the direction of Somerset Maugham. It happened that at just the time when Salinger was writing *Catcher,* Maugham was at the peak of his fame in the United States. He had sailed for America when (after his escape) his services were no longer needed in England, where, rather surprisingly, a house was specially built for him by his publisher Nelson Doubleday. In it he wrote *The Razor's Edge*, a huge bestseller at the end of the war.

Bertrand Russell at the Free Trade Hall

This novel drew fresh attention to his earlier autobiographical novel, *Of Human Bondage*. So well-known had *Of Human Bondage* become, in fact, that Holden Caulfield mentions both the book and its author. He rather dismisses Maugham as hardly the sort of writer you'd be desperate to phone after reading his novel - which is of course ironic, because there would have been no point at all in phoning, or writing a letter to, or trying to approach J D Salinger personally about *his* book, because as everyone knows he quickly became a total recluse. Maugham, by contrast, with the help of his secretary, continued to answer his readers' letters to the end of this days.

But Holden Caulfield did describe *Of Human Bondage* as "a pretty good book and all", and I needed no stronger incentive than that to turn to its author. I soon found myself devouring Maugham's books much as I had been devouring Russell's (all were available in Penguin in those days). That's how it tends to be with me.

*

W Somerset Maugham (1874-1965) was an unlikely writer, I suppose, ever to imagine as a literary hero. In so far as I knew much about him when I first started reading him, he wasn't an attractive figure. He was small and rather ugly, with a bad stammer which he never altogether succeeded in curing. One wonders how he would have coped with the publicity rounds required of writers today. It was the likely reason why he became a writer, the men in his family having usually adopted the legal profession. After his death it came out that he had been predominantly homosexual, at a time when it was both illegal and unmentionable - which was no joke. His middle brother Henry, a failed writer and also homosexual, had long ago committed suicide by swallowing nitric acid. So, with the increasing commercial success of his books, Somerset Maugham had settled on the French Riviera for an easier life in the late 1920s - though also because his secretary and male companion of the time, Gerald Haxton, had been barred from Britain following an offence against public decency.

None of this was known, however, to the general public in the early 1960s, nor for that matter to me. It's amazing how such things could once be hushed up. At the Villa Mauresque, Maugham entertained the most celebrated persons of the day, Sir Winston Churchill and the Duke and Duchess of Windsor included. He enjoyed his wealth, though, as he once explained, by the standards of the Riviera he was actually a rather poor millionaire.

But if I'm making him seem a stuffy and unpleasant sort of man, he certainly had a sense of humour. Once, when Noel Coward was due, as a practical joke, he told his other guests that Noel had lost all his money because his recent plays had flopped and he had made certain unwise investments. At the same time, on a very hot day, he instructed his staff, who included one of the best chefs on the Riviera, to feed him generous helpings of hot food as the poor man was starving. Expressing insistent sympathy that someone he didn't wish to talk to had lost his money was a method he used to deflect the attentions of such people - though of course Noel Coward was a friend.

Unpleasant and stuffy are words that would be better applied to his eldest brother, Frederic Herbert Maugham, who had a distinguished legal career and became Lord Chancellor in the 1930s, retiring with a peerage. On one rare visit to the Villa Mauresque he scarcely uttered a civil word, though he evidently had a sense of humour, too. Asked if he was enjoying his visit, he nodded, explaining that the plain cooking suited him very well.

*

In a preface to *Of Human Bondage* written for the collected edition of his works in the '30s, Maugham admits that, looking back, he himself found it difficult to separate fact from fiction. It was the first novel I read which faced religion squarely - and rejected it. In a painful early chapter, Philip Carey, an orphan with a club foot, is assured by his uncle, the Vicar of Blackstable (based on Whitstable) that faith can move mountains. Poor Philip embarks on a period of intense prayer, kneeling with bare knees on the hard floorboards of his bedroom as he implores God to cure him of his handicap. Of course it doesn't work. Instead, on the morning on which he has asked for the miracle to happen - having expected to skip lightly down to breakfast - he has to limp miserably down the stairs as usual.

As mentioned, in real life Maugham was born in France - in fact in Paris, in the British Embassy. His family origins were in England, and this was so that he would have British citizenship. He lived in the city until his mother died from tuberculosis when he was eight, soon to be followed by his father. He was then abruptly sent across the channel to Whitstable, into the care of the vicar of the town and his wife, a cold, middle-aged couple. With a new first language to cope with as well, there has been speculation that his stammer - his equivalent of Philip Carey's club foot - started at that time, and it is likely that he prayed to be cured like Philip. (Gore Vidal asserts, incidentally, in a somewhat ungenerous introduction to a Modern Library edition of *Of Human Bondage*, that Maugham's real handicap was his homosexuality.) He kept a photograph of his beloved mother on his bedside table for the rest of his life.

Maugham's religious attitude isn't confined to one book. In a very early novel, *Mrs Craddock,* he had also taken an uncompromising stand against it. There is an electrifying moment when the heroine, having just lost her baby in agonising labour, is urged to go to church to ask for God's forgiveness (to be "churched", as it's called). She cries out that it is God who should ask for *her* forgiveness! But such passages were thought far too scandalous for the time (1902), and had to be removed before *Mrs Craddock* could be accepted for publication. They weren't reinstated until decades later.

Ours wasn't a religious family. I barely knew what churches were for as a boy, and on the rare occasions (I think we were taken to church a few times from school) when I entered one, they seemed alien places. But I picked up that you must certainly never say a swear word in church - nor even think what you wanted to think, for that matter. You had to be perfectly well-behaved, clean, tidy and quiet. I didn't like this at all and came to resent the automatic respectability that seemed to be conferred on churchgoers. So later, when I read first Bertrand Russell then Somerset Maugham on the subject, I was surprised to discover that religion could in fact be attacked openly in print. Such apparent daring was rather thrilling to me, and any writer who did it was immediately a sort of kindred spirit, at least.

But there's a lot more to *Of Human Bondage* in particular than that. It's a mature novel, rich in ideas and with a deep understanding of human nature. It is mainly concerned not with religion but with the degradation of unrequited love, and that for me was again something of a first. Philip, now a modestly well-to-do medical student, falls helplessly in love with a worthless young waitress. Today, the author's bisexual nature has to be brought into any discussion of this fictional misery, though the protracted agony will read distressingly like the real thing to anyone who has suffered in that way. I know I first read the book myself when I was in the middle of a crush on a girl at work that was going nowhere. There was no real comparison, but I was certainly able to identify with poor Philip, dragging his club foot in pursuit of the hateful Mildred Rogers.

Despite his homosexual leanings, Maugham could certainly write about heterosexual relationships in a pretty convincing way, in *Of Human Bondage* and elsewhere. In fact he had a number of quite serious and prolonged affairs with women, and even married and had a child, before settling down to a homosexual life surprisingly late in the day. Gore Vidal writes of Maugham's "self-pity, which was to come to a full, rather ghastly flowering in *Of Human Bondage*". I dare say it can be read that way. For me, though, the novel is above all painfully honest.

*

Somerset Maugham wrote other excellent novels. He trained as a doctor (like Philip), and his very first book, *Liza of Lambeth* (1897), was drawn from material gathered in the slums, where only a doctor's black bag ensured his safety. Its success immediately won him over to letters - which he later sometimes regretted, for a doctor's work allowed him to see deeper into human souls, when the patient's guard was down. *Cakes and* Ale, with characters modelled controversially on Hugh Walpole and Thomas Hardy, goes over some of the same boyhood ground as *Of Human Bondage,* but it's a good deal lighter and funnier. Critics are apt to refer to it as his best book. Maugham insisted for years that the character of Alroy Kear wasn't intended to be Walpole, only admitting the truth after the latter's death.

The Moon and Sixpence, inspired by the life of Paul Gauguin (and another contender for Maugham's best book) tells the tragic story - tragic for those he comes into contact with - of Charles Strickland, a dull London stockbroker who to the astonishment of his family and friends gives it all up to paint in Paris. Later, like Gauguin, he sails for Tahiti. The book is rather unfair to Gauguin, incidentally, who was a more dutiful husband than is commonly supposed, and whose wife turned her back on *him*.

These novels both have a first-person narrator, and blend events of Maugham's real life with those of a fictional story. It was a method which matured fully in his many short stories. With its resulting distinctive narrator voice, it became his chief claim to originality, I would say. In *The Razor's Edge* he used his own name as narrator, and even went so far as to claim that he was telling a true story. This was perhaps a little *too* unfair on the reader.

But his most acclaimed short story, "Rain", is told in the third person. A group of ship's passengers is marooned in Pago Pago in the middle of a prolonged rainy season. They include a missionary and a prostitute, and the story revolves around the missionary's determined efforts to cure the woman of sin through the power of prayer. In a weakened condition (he has a more practical hold over her), she submits to a process of spiritual cleansing, abandoning her normally provocative attire for more modest garments. Then one morning, after a particularly heavy prayer session the previous night, she reverts suddenly to type, yelling to everyone that men - the missionary included - are all filthy pigs!

Ashenden (his spy book) is told in the third person, too, though the surname is the same as the one used in *Cakes and Ale*. It was certainly famous and influential in its day, but after James Bond is no doubt too lacking in fantasy nonsense for today's readers. Instead, it gives a more authentic account of the life of a spy. Maugham was apparently a figure of importance in the network, for when the turbulence in the country was at its height he was sent to Russia with an enormous sum of money on a futile mission to try to prevent the Bolshevik revolution. Exposure to the elements and other hardships - first in Switzerland, then Russia – resulted in his contracting tuberculosis. He spent a long period in a sanatorium in the north of Scotland, where he was evidently cured. He got a story out of the experience, too - called "Sanatorium". It was included in one of a couple of films of the 1940s - *Trio* and *Quartet* - with Michael Rennie in the lead. The films are available on DVD.

The best of his travel books is *Don Fernando* - about Spain in its Golden Age. Early on there is an extended translation of the Spiritual Exercises of Saint Ignatius Loyola, the founder of the Jesuits. Anyone interested in the workings of the medieval mind will be fascinated by the descriptions of the torments of Hell, upon which the penitent was required to meditate. Graham Greene considered *Don Fernando* his best book.

*

I never saw Somerset Maugham in the flesh, though his face appeared frequently in the papers in the '40s and '50s and was certainly familiar to me. When I began my own modest attempts at writing, I learned from him - as a young man, of course, with precious little relevant education - that a plain style was sufficient and there was no need to strain for more. I dare say I also picked up - albeit unconsciously - a fair amount about storytelling technique.

Of course, as I've said, when I was young, I knew little about the *real* W Somerset Maugham. When I learned that he was predominantly homosexual I was mildly surprised. Far more disturbing have been the references I've since come across to the procuring of "boys" during his travels to exotic places. It's mentioned in Gore Vidal's preface to *Of Human Bondage*. He wasn't alone, I imagine, among wealthy English travellers of the period, but it does sound pretty unsavoury all the same, tarnishing his reputation as a wise raconteur. One wonders if it could in some degree explain why, having once been so famous and popular (he sold forty million books in his lifetime) he is comparatively neglected today. In so far as I have ever allowed a writer's private life to influence my attitude to his work, Somerset Maugham has certainly been my own biggest challenge.

But *boys*? They surely mean young *men*.

*

Bertrand Russell's last years could be viewed as exemplary. He remained active - and right, too, particularly on the issues of nuclear weapons and the Vietnam war. Who now argues that nuclear weapons can actually be *used*, rather than simply held as a deterrent? Who now says that the American action in Vietnam was a good thing? But he also concerned himself with other issues. This went on, quite literally, until the day he died, for he dictated a statement on the situation in the Middle-East before he took to his bed for the last time.

Somerset Maugham's last years were less happy. There were the "rejuvenation" injections at the clinic of Dr Niehans in

Switzerland, which involved cells scraped from the still warm flesh of lamb fetuses. He was a confessed hedonist (he's been described as the first hippy), embittered now by the impairment of his faculties and the loss of such vital pleasures as extensive travelling, and finally reading. He worked for as long as he was able, but the only late book that made a noise was *Looking Back*, in which he launched a bitter attack on his late wife Syrie. It was serialised in the *Sunday Express*, but was otherwise denied publication in Britain. Then there were the bitter public squabbles over his prospective will, involving his daughter Liza and his secretary Alan Searle (who replaced Gerald Haxton after the war - he having died of various excesses). And worst of all there is a bizarre tale of his once defecating on the carpet in front of guests.

These things, as well as a realisation from obituary notices and other sources that in the eyes of the critics he was regarded as a writer only of the "second division", also put me off Maugham retrospectively. So I was pleased not long ago to read a fairly recent biography, by an American writer, Jeffrey Meyers, which puts his final years and literary reputation in a somewhat better light.

The defecating incident had no foundation whatever, for instance, while Searle had an inclination to exaggerate the grimness of later life at the Villa Mauresque for his own purposes. Regarding Maugham's position in English letters, it was quite heartening to read how influential he had once been with such younger writers as VS Naipaul, Anthony Burgess, and also George Orwell, who was an assiduous student to the point of copying whole sentences from Maugham's works. Evelyn Waugh, too, recognised his narrative skill, while Maugham influenced even OH Lawrence. Meyers indicates certain points of similarity between *Lady Chatterley's Lover* and *Mrs Craddock,* though Lawrence's novel was inevitably more explicit.

They had a brief, unhappy encounter in Mexico. Lawrence, who was having some difficulty at the time getting his own books published, despised the older writer for his commercial success, and for much else besides. Critical opinion (Meyers' included) now accepts automatically that he was by far the greater writer. I would only ask why the rest of us, reading simply for pleasure, should be expected to see writers that way, with greatness decided by some arbitrary authority. One might as well be back in school. Novelists don't write their novels with critical study in mind, but to be read, and reading is a one-to-one experience. What ought to matter is what a free-minded reader can find for himself in a writer. And as a young man, scholars would doubtless be shocked to hear, I found more in Somerset Maugham than I ever did in DH Lawrence.

Nowadays I've noticed that, with a good many other writers close enough on the shelves to choose from, I tend to dip into his books most often over breakfast. (So *somebody* is still reading him, forty-five years after his death!) I think what I like best at that time of day is a writer who draws you quietly into his world. There is also a self-deprecating tone in his writing which I find attractive and a total absence of pomposity. Was that the secret of his success? Here he is, starting a late essay entitled "Prose and Doctor Tillotson":

I looked with misgiving at the thinnish parcel that lay on the hall table with the letters that had come by the morning's post. I guessed what it contained. Like all authors who have achieved a certain notoriety, I am sent manuscripts by strangers who ask me to tell them what I think of their productions and, not seldom, beg me to use such influence as I may have to get them published. I regard them with a pang…

Perfect breakfast reading, for me at any rate! (The book turns out to be something entirely different, of course. It is a very old volume, sent to Maugham by a reader because of something he happened to have written, with the very old title *Maxims and Discourses, Moral and Divine, Taken from the Works of Arch-Bishop Tillotson, and Methodized and Connected.*)

His latest biographer - well, I believe there has been an even more recent book, focusing on Maugham's private life (I glimpsed a newspaper headline, with suitable photograph, a little while ago, asking the question: *WAS THIS THE MOST DEBAUCHED MAN OF THE 20th CENTURY?)* - stresses his great kindness and generosity. He left his future royalties - after Searle's death, that is - to the Royal Literary Fund, for example, which helps needy authors. In support of his subject, Meyers quotes Boswell on Dr Johnson: There was a "genuine humanity and real kindness in this great man, who has been most unjustly represented as altogether harsh and destitute of tenderness". For a biographer to try to put straight some of the unfairness heaped posthumously on a subject makes a refreshing change, though I realise that that isn't what sells books in the modern world.

Somerset Maugham kept his sardonic humour right to the end, too. I remember on the occasion of his ninetieth birthday his being asked by a television reporter what he thought of all the flowers well-wishers had sent him.

"I get the feeling of being in a cemetery," came the wintry reply.

4
A CONFEDERACY OF DUNCES

My general rule for choosing writers to write about here is that, in a long reading life, I must have picked up a great deal about them and their books without conscious effort. Or in other words my interest in them has to be entirely genuine rather than for study purposes. In most cases it's a process that began long ago, because these things take time. But now I am coming to a book and a writer I have read only relatively recently. This writer has nevertheless become something of a hero, too, though I know little about him beyond the barest facts. And in truth, it might be more accurate to say that it is his *mother* who should be my real hero.

*

A Confederacy of Dunces is the title of a novel - the story of one man against the world. It was written by an undiscovered young writer who was himself struggling against the blindness and stupidity of editors and others in the literary world who refused to see that his book was a work of genius. But the title could also (at least for me) express the rage and resentment felt by all writers engaged in the same kind of battle. (And let me quickly add that their judgement of themselves and their work is almost invariably wrong.) *A Confederacy of Dunces* is a cautionary tale for anyone setting out to be a writer. But first the novel - though it hardly needs me to speak up for it now.

It is set exclusively in New Orleans in the early 1960s. Whilst told in the third person, the novel is dominated by the extraordinary personality and presence of the leading character, Ignatius J Reilly, a creature with no known literary antecedents whom words are scarcely adequate to describe. A few that might be employed to that purpose are *grotesque, gargantuan, hypersensitive, repulsive, confrontational, self-absorbed, hypochondriacal, learned* and *brave*. The book doesn't burrow into the events and possible traumas of his early life that might explain him. We are expected to accept the man as he is, in relatively early adulthood, utterly impossible in every department of his life.

And yet Ignatius is a young man with a mission, a rather large one. Handicapped by his great size and general unsuitability for any kind of useful employment - or even recreational activity - this unlikely crusader is at war with the entire world as it has developed since the dawn of the Enlightenment. Sin and other offences against his idiosyncratic moral code are all around him. He is drawn frequently to the cinema, there to fulminate against the iniquities being enacted on the screen. He leads his poor uneducated mother the most terrible kind of dance (and the reader can't help wondering about parallels in the author's own life), opposing her tiniest efforts to make her life endurable. The casual jobs he manages to find, all far beneath the potential of a college graduate, he treats with a kind of unconscious contempt, wrecking all about him while believing himself to be driven by a higher purpose - or else falling back into self-pity over his troublesome and allegedly incapacitating pyloric valve, which appears to be never fully open and threatens to shut off altogether. The nearest he has to a girlfriend is an old college acquaintance, Myrna Minkoff. Myrna has a cause of her own, more in tune with the spirit of the times, but also a genuine concern for the man's mental and emotional welfare. In letters to him from distant places she recommends sex as a cure for his ills. Her urgings are savagely rebuffed.

Reilly dominates the novel, but some of the best comic episodes involve him only indirectly - for example the constant and deadly serious sniping between Lana Lee, the proprietor of the *Night of Joy* house of somewhat ill-repute, and her black floor sweeper, a young man known only as Jones. Then there are the trials of Patrolman Mancuso, charged with - and always failing - to bring in some weirdos. Or again the hilarious conversations between Mancuso's subversive Aunt Santa and Ignatius's mother. Best of all, though, are the domestic squabbles between Mr and Mrs Levy over the future of *Levy Pants* - briefly Reilly's employer - and the decrepit and grotesque but as yet unretired Miss Trixie. I can't tell if the accents - white and black - in which the dialogues are conducted are fully authentic, but they add immensely to the comedy.

*

Some novels have the power to make you smile and now and then even laugh out loud as you read them. This novel can have that same effect long after putting it down. It won a Pulitzer Prize and is now recognised and well-established as a modern classic of American literature. Yet the young author, John Kennedy Toole, saw none of this. He had committed suicide long before the book was taken up. We owe it to his mother that we have the book at all. Only her extraordinary persistence finally forced it into print, *ten years after her son's death.*

As with all the arts, striving to achieve the big breakthrough in the literary field is a desperate business. I'd had some experience of it myself, in my own modest writing life, before I ever discovered this book. But it came as a deep shock to realise that even a genius like John Kennedy Toole could fail. Nevertheless, I wouldn't expect any undiscovered young writer who happens to read these words to give up the struggle. I haven't yet given it up myself, after all, and I'm into old age! But one thing I *did* decide after reading *A Confederacy of Dunces* - and it's the chief reason why I'm bringing it into the picture here - was that it was madness to go on trying too hard to please publishers, editors, or agents. After all, books were in decline, in the new age of computers and the internet. From now on I would stick to a policy of writing what I pleased. The result would very likely be better, in any case. But if it still turned out that nobody wanted what I'd written, too bad. At least I would have enjoyed myself.

Which is precisely what I'm doing right now!

5
THE BROTHER

Most people do it, but reading a writer's best stuff first is apt to spoil you for the rest of their work. ff, for example, you start with PG Wodehouse's wonderfully funny *Jeeves* stories, his other books can be a bit of a struggle to get through afterwards. Often readers don't get beyond a writer's best-known book. I try to be more persistent, though it doesn't always work out. Take the Irish humorist Flann O'Brien. Again, contrary to the general idea of this book, I don't know much about him. Nor have I managed to read more than a small part of his output. Happily, though, it's a part that has delighted me as much as anything I've so far encountered in my journey through books.

Flann O'Brien was a pen name - his real name was Brian O'Nolan. But he also had a second pen name, which he used for a long-running column in the *Irish Times:* Myles na Gopaleen. His best known novel is probably *The Third Policeman*. That's what I'd picked up, anyway, back some time in the '70s. I expected to read it and then move onto the rest of his books, as I usually do. But I couldn't for some reason immediately find a copy.

I did, however, come across a volume called *The Best of Myles* by Flann O'Brien/Myles na Gopaleen. It was of course a collection of short pieces, the sort of thing I was finding I increasingly enjoyed, for if you're into writing yourself it does sap your reading stamina. Novels can seem like too much trouble. So, taking a chance, I bought a copy of *The Best of Myles* instead.

The pieces were culled from his column in the *Irish Times*, which he started in 1940, though it seems to have had no special connection with the Second World War. The book opens with a section called "Waama, etc" (a reference to the Irish Writers, Actors, Artists, Musicians Association), which I found amusing enough, although as the book ran to nearly four hundred pages I was already wondering how far I was going to get with it. Luckily, it didn't take me long to reach something that was altogether more captivating, for only thirty pages into the collection I came upon *The Brother*.

I was reminded of Flann O'Brien and *The Brother* by a piece in the *Guardian* Saturday Review. A book of his called *The Various Lives of Keats and Chapman, and The Brother* had been re-issued. I already knew of it because I had a copy, bought long ago - direct from the publishers, sight unseen, which shows how keen I was to get my hands on more of the stuff I'd discovered in *The Best* of *Myles*.

But the book had been a disappointment. I had thought the stuff I already knew was a mere selection, and that I would surely find a great deal more of it in this new book. Most of *The Various Lives*, however, was devoted to the adventures of Keats and Chapman, which set up punch lines consisting of sometimes less than hilarious puns. The whole thing was derived from Keats' poem "On First Looking into Chapman's Homer", which O'Brien/Myles interpreted amusingly as a pigeon.

The Brother of *The Various Lives* refers to a play. It is funny enough to read and I would love to see it staged, but it simply isn't the same thing as the original stuff. The humour there is of the more literary kind. As with PG Wodehouse, it's all to do in the choice and arrangement of words on the page.

Brian Darwent

*

My late wife was no more ready to feel enthusiastic about my enthusiasms than most wives (and I appreciate that it's no different the other way), but I remember a miserable wet family holiday afternoon in the '70s that was saved by *The Brother*. We were staying in what had been advertised as a farm cottage in Somerset, but which had turned out to be a conventional red-brick semi-detached house. The children were bored, and outside it was pouring with rain. With little money to spend on the kind of indoor entertainment that might be available, we were confined to the house. I had with me *The Best of Myles,* which I had been chuckling loudly over in bed, and embarked on a desperate attempt to relieve the gloom and tedium by reading aloud for everyone from the section devoted to *The Brother*.

And it worked! My wife soon grabbed the book off me and took over. We had a marvellous time with it. Even our two girls seemed to find the stuff side-splittingly funny, and the youngest was no more than four at the time. After an hour or so the sun came out at last and we set off outdoors, refreshed and happy. *The Brother* can work miracles!

The pieces are column length, with a slow build up, so it isn't easy to illustrate the humour with a short extract. They consist of one-sided conversations at a Dublin bus stop between a loquacious Irishman and a rather pompous Englishman, whose presence in such a setting is never explained. The conversations are entirely concerned with the goings on in a local "digs", the lives of whose guests (or inmates) are dominated to the point of tyranny by *The Brother*. Here, the tyrant has decided for no good reason to grow a beard - which seems harmless enough, though it causes great consternation:

- The digs was in the front line for near on a fortnight.

- No doubt your relative was the author of this tension?

- Tuesday fortnight was 0-Day. The brother comes down to breakfast without the mark of a shavin' razor on his jaw… Of course the crowd starts eatin' and takin' no notice. There would be no question of anybody passin' remarks, you know. There was very ferocious eatin' gain' on that morning… The next morning the crowd is sittin' at the table as white as a sheet. Begob, you would think they were all for the firin' squad. And down comes the brother… The face was as black as a black-faced goat. There was hair on him from the ears to the neck… I couldn't tell you how the crowd in the digs lived through the next ten days… Do you know what? If the brother came down without a face on him at all, there wouldn't be wan that would pass a remark …

But then I can only count Flann O'Brien/Myles Na Gopaleen as one of my minor heroes. Making me laugh, even out loud, hardly counts as a real act of literary heroism.

6
REVIVING SAROYAN

I used to live quite close to a huge Borders bookshop near Ellesmere Port in Cheshire - now sadly closed and empty, and it seemed to be doing so *well*. It's the kind of tragedy we book lovers will have to get used to. The place was well-stocked - it was like a barn - but most of the time there was only a single title to be found on the fiction shelves by the American writer William Saroyan (pronounced SaROY'n), and I had helped to put it there myself. It was a skimpy little collection of short stories, *Fresno Stories*, published by New Directions in New York.

The little paperback could be hard to locate, too, hidden as it often was alphabetically amongst all the copies of JD Salinger's small number of actual titles. What a turn up for the books! as they say. Saroyan had been so very much more prolific, besides once being vastly more famous. I used to prop the book up on the shelf, facing potential customers, and hiding as many as I could of the Salinger spines. I'm not saying I'm proud of the fact, but I could by now be the only person in Britain - maybe even in the world - who knows that Salinger was influenced by Saroyan, and could indicate certain minor points of similarity (Holden Caulfield/Homer Macauley, for example, and the fact that both books have a character called Ackley) between Salinger's *The Catcher in the Rye* and Saroyan's first and best-known novel, *The Human Comedy*, very different as the two books otherwise are.

His career followed something of a sky-rocket trajectory, but he was by no means forgotten when I was first rummaging in Percival's. I have since read that at around that time it was rumoured that two Californian writers were under consideration for the Nobel Prize. It wouldn't be hard to guess that one of them was John Steinbeck, and he did win the prize in 1962. William Saroyan was thought to be the other, although he had no time for literary prizes. In the late '30s he had turned down a Pulitzer for his second play, *The Time of Your Life* (revived in the early 1980s by the RSC, with John Thaw in the lead), because he detested the idea of Art being patronised by Money. He may well have turned down the Nobel Prize, too. It's hard to believe now - particularly in Britain, where his books have now been out of print for decades - but his name really was once right up there with Steinbeck, Hemingway and the rest of the literary big beasts of the '30s and '40s.

*

William Saroyan was an ethnic Armenian - born in Fresno, California, in 1908, his family and neighbours refugees from the Turkish troubles of that time back in the homeland. His father Armenak, a failed preacher and poet, died from peritonitis when he was only three, as a consequence of which he spent several years in an orphanage. Self-taught, determined to make up for his father's failure in the New World, displaying a youthful disregard for the conventions of writing, and expressing open contempt for money interests from the start, Saroyan sprang to fame in 1934 with a ground-breaking collection of short stories written in the depths of the Depression, *The Daring Young Man on the Flying Trapeze*, when he was twenty-six. The book's title had no special connection with the song. He simply used it as a metaphor for the daring launch, in such unfavourable circumstances, of his career as a professional writer. ("Start your career on the right note," he would later advise a young Armenian poet.)

And the launch was indeed spectacular. Overnight, he became the most talked-about new writer in America. The book has lasted, too. New Directions have had *The Daring Young Man on the Flying Trapeze* in print again in recent times, seventy years after its first appearance, albeit with an old-fashioned circus trapeze artist for a cover illustration.

Many more short-story collections - his preferred literary form and the one he probably did most to influence - would follow through the '30s *(Inhale and Exhale, Little Children, Love Here is My Hat, The Trouble with Tigers, Peace It's Wonderful)*. Saroyan's method was improvisatory. He composed straight on the typed page, at full speed, in a state of intense concentration. And it was just the same when he turned later to writing novels and plays. He claimed to have written *The Time of Your Life* in six days, *The Human Comedy* in eleven.

That first novel began life as a film - starring Mickey Rooney as the boy delivering wartime telegrams - the screenplay winning Saroyan an Oscar. The novel followed. It was a bestseller during the war, while *The Time of Your Life* had earlier been a Broadway hit - where it first brought Gene Kelly to prominence as Harry the Hoofer. Another popular success in that same period was *My Name is Aram*, a collection of short stories presenting in a poetical light his early life (after the orphanage years) in the midst of the Armenian community settled in California's San Joaquin Valley. Saroyan was among the first American authors to write about the immigrant experience, and *My Name is Aram* probably remains his best book of all. It too has had a long life in print in America.

But all that was changing. He had met and quickly married a very young society girl, Carol Marcus - whose friends included Oona O'Neill and Gloria Vanderbilt - and was almost immediately called up for war service and sent to London, attached to the Signal Corps. As a famous - and for the moment wealthy-writer, he appears to have had a pretty easy time of it there. At one point he was able to occupy a room, with service, in the Savoy Hotel, where the army brass expected him to write a novel to promote Anglo-American relations. He had left his young wife pregnant, and on its completion he was promised leave to visit her and his baby son in New York. But Saroyan was no more a lover of the army, even in wartime, than the business world. He produced instead an anti- war novel, *The Adventures of Wesley Jackson*, for which daring he came close to being court-martialled. His promised leave was forgotten.

Back in America, in the immediate post-war years, he recklessly gambled away most of his enormous earnings from his big bestsellers. Not that he could easily help himself. It was a lifelong compulsive habit, reflecting his headlong approach to life. And gambling was always at the heart of his writing, too. He trusted totally to luck. Instead of picking up where he had left it, however, his literary career now plummeted. His 1949 collection of stories, *The Assyrian*, sold only 4000 copies. New writers like James Jones, Norman Mailer and Irwin Shaw, were coming through, with a different kind of war experience altogether, and a much greater willingness to write about it in a way that would please publishers - and readers. Saroyan found himself out of fashion, and in the meantime his marriage had been going from bad to worse.

Although thoroughly incompatible, he and Carol (who may well have been the model for Holly Golightly in Truman Capote's *Breakfast at Tiffany's*) were married twice and divorced twice. She later married Walter Matthau. Embittered and still in love with her, Saroyan moved to Europe, settling finally in an apartment in Paris. He would spend twenty years there, at least in the summer months. He later bought a second home in Fresno for mainly winter use.

*

Fresno Stories was partly drawn from his successful early period, some of the stories having already appeared in an earlier posthumous anthology entitled *The Man with the Heart in the Highlands,* which I compiled (as will be seen). They used to stock that in Border's, too. The only reason *Fresno Stories* survived for longer on the shelves was because I myself bought a copy from time to time, and they got replaced. I would pass the books on to friends, who appeared to like the stuff, although no William Saroyan revival resulted. I had been waiting for such an event for some time.

In his heyday, and beyond, he was enormously influential, inspiring several generations of unschooled young men equipped, as he had once been, with little more than cigarettes, coffee, a battered old typewriter, and a burning belief that they had something to say. A fair number of them, like Salinger (another was Jack Kerouac), became famous in their own right, although the great majority were destined to remain obscure - but it rarely stopped them writing. By the 1970s, though, the novels of his middle period (Rock *Wagram, The Laughing Matter, Mama I Love You, Boys and Girls Together, One Day in the Afternoon of the World*) having failed to win back for him his former position with either the critics or the general reading public, Saroyan's new books were no longer making it into print in Britain.

I myself discovered him quite late in the day, yet he had the same effect on me as on earlier generations. I remember stumbling upon *The Daring Young Man* in Percival's and starting to read the first story, called "Seventy-Thousand Assyrians" (it led Joseph Heller to make Yossarian an Assyrian in *Catch-22)*. I didn't have to read very far before resolving to buy a typewriter myself. He not only inspired me to write, he turned me instantly into a writing addict. William Saroyan is more responsible than anyone - Russell, Maugham, Thurber, Steinbeck, or any of the other writers I was discovering in those years - for the fact that I am still writing today, as obscure as ever. Poorly-gifted as you might feel yourself to be, he had a way of persuading you that you too could be a writer.

*

Fabers had published Saroyan in hardback for twenty-five years, up until 1960, but they kept him in print in their paper-covered editions through to the mid-1970s, before dropping him altogether. Other London publishers (Cassell, Michael Joseph, Peter Davies) had also briefly taken him on. But now, in the late '70s, he was finally out of print here.

Others may have noticed this minor literary calamity, but none of them reacted as I did. I determined to make it my mission to rescue this "wonderful writer" (as Keith Waterhouse once described him) from the obscurity into which he was now apparently sinking. A new anthology of his best writings was long overdue. I aimed to be its editor. But I can't pretend that my motives were selfless. Wouldn't such a volume put my name on the cover of a book at last, besides allowing me to contribute a lengthy introduction.

My own writing efforts hadn't been going very well, you see. They had been going nowhere, in fact. Most fledgling writers start with short stories, but by the early 1960s there was no longer much of a market for these - whereas in Saroyan's day, despite the Depression, there had been lots of glossy magazines in America publishing them. I had a full-time job as well - while he had seemed able to live on money earned gambling, plus the little he got for working on his uncle's fruit-and-vegetable market stall at weekends. I was soon married, too, with children and full domestic responsibilities - compared with the single life he had, occupying a small rented room. And living in Warrington, in fairly easy times, I had little in the way of raw material - while he had been living in San Francisco, with the effects of the Depression all around him, besides having his early life among the Armenians and other immigrant communities trying to make a go of it on the wrong side of the tracks to draw on. We were both self-taught, it's true, but his self-education seemed to be complete by his early twenties, whereas mine remains ongoing even today. In short, there was never a chance that I would be able to follow his earlier example. But now, with this new anthology idea, I could see a way of getting my own back, as you might say.

I had been collecting British editions of Saroyan's books for a long time, and was fortunate to have a friend living in New York who could hunt there for titles that hadn't crossed the Atlantic. So, researching the book didn't require as much labour as might be imagined. Soon I was ready to write to the man himself with my proposal. I knew he was still spending his summers in his Paris apartment, well away from the heat of Fresno - not to mention the long reach of the American income-tax authorities - at work at this late stage in his career chiefly on a series of randomly arranged memoirs, with titles like *Days of Life and Death and Escape to the Moon*, *Places Where I've Done Time*, and *Letters from 74 Rue Taitbout, or, Don't Go But If You Must Say Hello to Everybody*. In photographs from this later period, with a huge moustache, receding hair and noble brow, he had begun to cultivate the appearance of an Armenian patriarch.

Bertrand Russell at the Free Trade Hall

Disappointingly, there was no quick reply. I thought my work had been in vain - but then I returned from holiday that year (1979) to find a letter on my doormat from the Laurence Pollinger agency in Mayfair. I learned that they represented Saroyan in Europe and he had passed on my letter. At first they were suspicious. I proposed a visit and met Gerald Pollinger, deep inside their offices in Maddox Street (off Regent Street). He was a very kind man, and, satisfied apparently that I wasn't some kind of charlatan, he granted me permission to pursue my idea, although it was made clear to me that I would have to make the running myself. (I met him several times afterwards and we were in touch by letter for a good many years. I only found out a few years ago that he had died. I don't believe they make literary agents like Gerald Pollinger anymore.)

I set about the task of finding a British publisher with enthusiasm. Saroyan seemed to me to be quite a major figure still. But the economic times were against me. The 1978/79 "Winter of Discontent" was followed by the election of Mrs Thatcher, and soon we were in the middle of the deepest recession since the war. Publishers felt the pinch like everyone else. For them it now had to be bestsellers or nothing. I spent well over a year approaching the most likely ones, receiving polite messages of sympathy only.

In desperation, fully expecting a rebuff, I asked for permission to try America, a territory I imagined to be well stitched up by others. Gerald Pollinger approached Saroyan - and to my surprise a positive message came quickly back. He even offered advice on which publishers were best avoided. Evidently, he was taking a close interest in my project.

By now, though, America was following Britain's economic lead. To general disbelief, Mrs Thatcher's soulmate, the former

B-movie actor Ronald Reagan, had been elected president, and the same destructive policies were already being applied. So the response from publishers was much the same. In fact the situation in America was rather worse, for (as I found out later) Saroyan had been making a habit of falling out, sometimes almost violently, with the very people in the publishing world over there who might have helped his cause.

*

But there was one last chance. In the early summer of 1981, I arranged to take my family on a holiday to New York, staying with the friend who had helped me with material. It might be a chance to call in and see prospective publishers while I was in town. I took my manuscript along anyway, just in case.

Well, as we were about to sit down to dinner on our first evening, the television news bulletin announced that William Saroyan had *died*. He had been suffering from cancer, it transpired, throughout the period of my labours. Next morning he was on the front page of the *New York Times,* with a full-page obituary notice inside. Talk about being in the right place at the right time! Shocked and saddened as I felt, I was of course on the phone at the first opportunity.

And this happened:

"Haven't we already turned that book down?" said Little, Brown (in Boston).

"Sorry, but the man's death and the obituary notices you mention make no real difference," said WW Norton, on Fifth Avenue.

"Little point in calling in," said Harcourt, Brace - happy publishers in better times of the big bestsellers, *The Human Comedy, My Name is Aram* and *The Time of Your Life*, plus many other successful titles.

Nothing had changed, it seemed.

Except that shortly before his death Saroyan had written to Gerald Pollinger (who hadn't known of his illness), telling him that he would soon be dead and making him his literary executor. It smoothed the way for me with the Armenian lawyers who were otherwise controlling the estate. The result was that *The New Saroyan Reader: A Connoisseur's Anthology of the Writings of William Saroyan, edited with an introduction by Brian Darwent* was eventually taken up by a publisher in California, Creative Arts. It came out in 1984. The reviews in America were good and the sales not bad. It was also distributed in Britain, and nicely reviewed by Robert Nye - a big Saroyan fan - in the *Guardian*. I made quite a bit of money, and it led to two further anthologies, one of which I've already mentioned, *The Man with the Heart in the Highlands*.

That was a very much easier task. I remember going into work one Saturday morning with a briefcase loaded with books, from which I made a selection as I stood there at the photocopier. I had posted the stuff off to New York by lunchtime. New Directions wouldn't accept *me* as official editor, though they did pay me around £500 for bringing the material to their attention (in fact I'd supplied it at their request) and put a little note at the front to that effect. Was a book ever in history assembled in such a way? And shortly after that I put together a selection of material from Saroyan's autobiographical writings. *Saroyan: Memoirs* was published in London, without fanfare. It was part of a deal involving a biography of Jack Trevor Story (of which more later). But then to my astonishment a Spanish publisher showed strong interest and brought it out in translation, in a handsome little hardcover edition. Once more I was surprisingly well rewarded. I devised other imaginative compilations as well, but none of them quite made it into print. The Saroyan bubble I had sought to keep inflated had sadly burst.

*

Emptying my loft long afterwards, I unearthed all the old correspondence connected with these projects. It included interesting letters from such writers as Kurt Vonnegut, Arthur Miller, Keith Waterhouse and Alan Sillitoe - all highly supportive. Most intriguing of all, though - if least helpful at the time - was a little card from Paris, with tiny, barely legible handwriting in black ink. It said:

> *Dear Mr Darwent,*
> *Thank you for your letter. I am not familiar with Saroyan's work & cannot help with your request.*
> *I am sorry to disappoint you.*
> *With best wishes for your project.*
> *Yours sincerely*
> *Samuel Beckett*

But what rather alarmed me was the amount of effort I had been willing to put into all this. There *was* a genuine minor Saroyan revival in America in 1984, marking the fiftieth anniversary of the publication of *The Daring Young Man on the Flying Trapeze*. Along with *The New Saroyan Reader*, there was a biography by Lawrence Lee and Barry Gifford, and an anthology of Saroyan's writings published in the Armenian magazine,

Hairenik, edited by Leo Hamalian. But since those days the man himself has inevitably fallen in my estimation as I've discovered more about the *real* William Saroyan.

In fact I began to find that out quite soon, for his son Aram quickly published a very bitter memoir, *Last Rites*, actually written while his father lay dying in hospital. Feelings would have had to be very bitter indeed for someone to do that - although the book did end with a final and very moving reconciliation. *Last Rites* was basically the story of every son of a famous father, the famous man's career always coming first, although in Saroyan's case his attempt at ordinary married life was also hampered by Old World ideas about the family and the position of women. And on top of those things, Aram suggests, his emotional life had been affected by a serious disturbance to his psyche, caused by the early death of his own father, right at the very beginning of his conscious life.

It also has to be said that although Saroyan had his devotees, and even champions (I'm thinking in particular of the great American theatre critic George Jean Nathan, whose strong support helped get him started as a playwright), there were also those who were dismissive, or worse, of his talent. Among his detractors were Ernest Hemingway, Joseph Heller and James Thurber. Annoyed by remarks about him in that early story, "Seventy-Thousand Assyrians", Hemingway responded with an aggressive piece in *Esquire*. (It's irrelevant, but in the story the narrator discovers that there are only seventy-thousand Assyrians left in the world.) Heller seems to have been offended by a satirical piece Saroyan published in *Playboy*, in which he took a few swipes at him and the other literary "upstarts" who were keeping him out the limelight. At any rate in his late novel, *Closing Time*, he took more than a few swipes at Saroyan, who by then had been dead for more than a decade. James Thurber gave one of his own books the title, *The Middle-Aged Man on the Flying Trapeze*. It contained a few parodies of famous writers of the day and he intended including Saroyan, although - as he confided in a letter to a friend at the time - the task had defeated him. I dare say the sentimentality in Saroyan's work - a frequent charge, which he struggled to rebut - is probably what got up Thurber's nose. (He criticised John Steinbeck's wartime novel *The Moon is Down* for similar reasons.) But Saroyan seemed unaware of Thurber's low opinion of him. He mentions the famous humorist here and there in his rambling memoirs with proper respect. They shared a table at a gathering of arts' people during one of Roosevelt's election campaigns. Later, he recalled only that he and Thurber had been alone in not shaking the president's hand.

I was pretty shocked when I discovered how Thurber felt, because I'd long been a fan of *his* work, too. But William Saroyan has nevertheless remained among my great heroes. The way he'd broken down the thick shut doors of the American publishing establishment with his first book will always ensure that. His most recent biographer, John Leggett, may have concluded that his talent wasn't sufficient to sustain a full career, but the fact is that he remained a professional writer, on his own terms, to the very end, approaching his *last* book, *Obituaries*, in a typical way. There was no research, nor any real forethought. He chanced upon *Variety's* list of the showbusiness dead for one year (1976), realised he had had some sort of acquaintance with quite a number of them, and decided to use it as the basis for a book - or, as he might have put it, to set his writing loose. If he hadn't known the person, he speculated about them, or made something up, typing only as far as the bottom of a single page. Not for him, either, the double-spacing you would expect in the manuscripts of a professional author. He typed single-spaced (I have seen an example) - always had done. And typically, he had to find a new publisher - which turned out to be Creative Arts, publishers five years later of *The New Saroyan Reader*. Nor was *Obituaries* a total flop. It came close to winning a National Book Award. I still have a copy on my shelves, along with all of his books. They make quite a collection. I'm wondering whom to leave them to!

In the meantime here's an extract to savour from an earlier memoir, *Not Dying,* also included in my anthology. (The piece was broadcast on Radio 4, incidentally, from *The New Saroyan* Reader.) Hal Francis was one of a number of "hungry young writers, fresh from poverty, fresh from the cold of the grubby neighbourhoods of the big cities of America", who in the 1930s found themselves working in Hollywood on movie scripts, and enjoying the life. But Hal hadn't yet published a novel, and he needed to - urgently - in order to impress his employers and thus stay in the movie business. The trouble was that he had met an altogether different kind of writer, Thomas Wolfe, and could no longer believe in his own writing:

…Hal believed that as *long* as *Thomas Wolfe was writing there was no reason in the world for him to write, too. Tom Wolfe* was *saying it all.*

He loved and admired Wolfe as *a giant of* a *man, voracious and insatiable, a compulsive writer who was* a*/ so inexhaustible, or very nearly* so… a *working writer who stayed in* a *dump of an apartment in Brooklyn, who worked with such intensity that he forgot time, forgot food and drink, and then after Jong hours of fierce and trance- like concentration,* and *the swiftest writing in the world… he staggered out of his hovel, his huge body purified by the fiery labour, his heavy body made light, almost weightless, by the passing* of *the hours, and he began* *to fly over the streets, crossing the bridge to Manhattan at three or four in the morning, finding men at work on the docks, joining them in their work for an hour* or *two, then flying on…*

Hal Francis was of course mistaken about Thomas Wolfe, at least a little, as Saroyan points out. And Hal was mistaken about himself, too. He *had* something to say, but not in writing. He said it at the bar, drinking. He needed someone to listen to him *now*, not later.

Which I dare say is the fundamental thing that makes other people different from writers.

7
KURT VONNEGUT AT CHELTENHAM

Kurt Vonnegut was one of those writers I'd heard of long before I read him. *Slaughterhouse-5*, his novel inspired by the fire-bombing of Dresden when he was a POW in the city, made an impact well beyond the book review pages, back in 1969. I didn't rush out to buy a copy, however. I thought it would be yet another macho war novel - the title certainly gave me that impression - and I was in the habit of never reading bestsellers on principle in any case. In fact I continued not to read him for almost twenty years. Then somehow I got to know that he had been the speaker at a memorial service in New York for William Saroyan in 1981(Henry Kissinger and Mayor Koch were also present), and I began to wonder about him. None of his subsequent books had made quite as big a splash - in fact I couldn't have named a single one of them off the top of my head. But I had picked up by now that he was an important writer, and the association with Saroyan was certainly intriguing. Maybe it was time at last to give Kurt Vonnegut a try.

I didn't start with *Slaughterhouse-5*, though. That would have been too obvious. Or perhaps, feeling that it must be his best book, I wanted to save it until I knew more about him. So I chose instead a novel that had come out soon afterwards: *Breakfast of Champions*. The book is crudely illustrated - by the author himself - and could be seen as sloppy and self-indulgent. But shining through, I saw at once, is a powerful moral attitude, present (I've since discovered) in all of Vonnegut's work. I also responded warmly to its black humour - which wasn't normally my favourite kind of writing. It contrasted with the author's simple style -

almost at times as if he was writing for children. In fact I found myself hooked once more. He virtually took over my reading life for the next several months, if not longer. Even today, two decades further on, his books are rarely out of my reach - and I do often reach for them. It's been as strong a reading obsession as has ever gripped me.

*

Vonnegut was interviewed on British television for an arts' programme a few months before he died in 2007. I knew that he was still alive then, at eighty-three, and yet it was hard not to be surprised. He'd chain-smoked all his life, in an almost suicidal way. The TV appearance was linked to a new book, a collection of random writings on the contemporary scene, entitled A *Man Without a Country*. It was also discussed at some length on *Newsnight Review*. Slight as the book is, it had its defenders, though an American guest whose name I didn't catch was dismissive. He said he was tired of these multi-millionaires with social consciences who needed *more* money. Hadn't Vonnegut announced in print that he had written his last book? (This was true. He had had a lot of difficulty with his novel *Timequake*, and it was in that context that he had declared in 1997 that it would be his last.) Furthermore, there had been a party at the Playboy Club to mark his retirement, the man went on to say. He hadn't written a decent novel since the far-off days of *Slaughterhouse-5* and *Breakfast of Champions*. Nor had his memoir-style books ever been any good. Why now inflict this pointless little volume on a long-suffering reading public?

Was the man right? It had never occurred to me to question Kurt Vonnegut's integrity, and I had to agree that *A Man Without a Country* didn't amount to very much. I didn't much like what I was hearing - and was especially troubled by the revelation of the Playboy Club party. But a reaction soon set in.

Vonnegut had the right to change his mind about his own writing plans, surely? He'd clearly been in an exasperated state of mind when making his announcement. But in any case, *A Man Without a Country* was by no means a worthless effort. He has a piece of practical advice for writers, for instance, which I have taken directly on board. Have you seen a semi-colon yet in this book? The answer is no, since there aren't any. This I got directly from A *Mon Without a Country,* and I believe it has definitely improved my writing style. Vonnegut says of the semi-colon, on page 23, 'They are transvestite hermaphrodites, representing absolutely nothing. All they do show is that you've been to college." And I never did go to college, did I? So his advice was especially appropriate in my case.

But there is also an important idea in the book which I hadn't seen expressed before. It has to do with the gravitation to positions of power of "psychotic personalities". This is a medical term - not something he'd made up. It refers to smart, personable people who have no conscience and can thus act decisively with no need to consider the consequences of what they do, since they don't care. This isn't a choice. There're *unable* to care, because they're *sick*. (Vonnegut refers to the classical medical text on psychotic personalities: *The Mask of Sanity,* by Dr Hervey Cleckley, and urges us to read it!) The results of the behaviour of these people had been clearly seen in the collapse of various giant corporations, their top executives pleading total innocence. (I do wonder, too, about the new breed of traders on the world's financial markets - those mathematical geniuses who now devise and set loose fiendishly complex computer programmes with no apparent concern about the likely future financial disasters they may be inviting.) Vonnegut suggests that such people are now close to the heart of the government of the United States itself. It's a serious flaw in the whole system of democracy, he tells us, never mind commerce. Even in his school days, he recalls, those who ran for class president were apt to be clearly disturbed.

Fascinating - and worrying - stuff!

As for the "multi-millionaire" tag, was Vonnegut really that wealthy? His books have sold well - but they were seldom filmed, which I imagine is where the real money is. Nor did he try earning money in other ways, after his first big success. He described himself as a "straight income man". Not the route to becoming a multi-millionaire, I fancy. I happen to have stood in front of his house in New York, too (this was before his death), and its location apart, it struck me as relatively modest. It wasn't some kind of mansion, that's for sure. (Curiously, it also looked to be empty.)

But the critic on *Newsnight Review* was suggesting, anyway, that *A Man Without a Country* had been cobbled together purely to make money. Really? Why would a multi-millionaire bother? I disagreed with him, too, on Vonnegut's previous memoir-style books. These were not *straight* memoirs. In them he published his speeches, commencement addresses, essays, humorous articles, book reviews, letters and the like, joined up with bits of what he called "connective tissue". *Palm Sunday* is my favourite. I dip into it constantly.

But what might really have got me reaching for my pen, if I hadn't given up on such bad habits, was the man's remark that Vonnegut hadn't written a decent novel since those distant days of *Slaughterhouse-5* and *Breakfast of Champions*. A case could be made for several - *Bluebeard, Deadeye Dick, Jailbird, Mother Night* - but the Kurt Vonnegut novel which stands out from the rest, published in 1986 and rivalling *Slaughterhouse-5* as his best ever, is surely *Galapagos*. He held that view himself.

It's a black satire on Darwin's *Theory of Evolution* - which despite being an agnostic and a humanist Vonnegut always had some difficulty accepting, since it was so heartless and cruel (a view of Darwin's work that doesn't seem to occur to many people). In the midst of a most dire world ecological and financial crisis a group of Earthlings, as the author liked to call human beings, of diverse and peculiar genetic inheritance, are left by chance as the only passengers on the "Nature Cruise of the Century", a special, highly publicised voyage to the Galapagos Islands, once intended for A-list celebrities. Their ship out of action, they become stranded among the blue-footed boobies and other animal oddities first encountered by Darwin on the Beagle.

Meanwhile things on the rest of the planet are going from bad to worse and beyond, so that these bizarre castaways become the human race's sole survivors. Their solitary piece of functioning technological equipment is a computer device called "Mandarax", which can answer any question and talk to them in many languages, but is of no practical use whatever. The first offspring, already showing signs of mutation, are born as a result of secretive mechanical insemination. Thus are the seeds sown. And over the next million years these last humans, adapting to their new environment, evolve into small-brained, seal-like creatures which can do no further harm to the planet. In the early '90s the *Guardian* published a piece of mine on *Galapagos* in their *I Wish I had Written…* series.

Brian Darwent

*

Vonnegut was born in Indianapolis in 1922, of German ancestry, though by then the anti-German propaganda of the First World War had caused his family to abandon German culture. He began selling stories in the late '40s to the glossy American magazines of the day. This success was short-lived, however, for the new medium of television soon started to draw away the advertising revenues supporting the short-story market. He had to return to earning a living from more mundane work. He was once, for instance, the manager of a Saab automobile dealership on Cape Cod (this is from *A Man Without a Country* again), trying to sell a solitary two-stroke model with certain bizarre features, such as "suicide doors opening into the slipstream". But he continued to write, and also to teach creative writing (John Irving was a student), his reputation slowly building until his big breakthrough came with *Slaughterhouse-5*.

As he tells in the autobiographical opening chapter, it was a novel he'd been at work on for a long time, from a variety of angles. He had only survived the destruction of Dresden because he and his fellow POWs were billeted in an underground slaughterhouse. They saw the city before and after. With such material, he had thought that writing a novel about it would be easy. Instead, he found himself blocked. The wife of an old army buddy he was visiting, looking for ideas, finally put him on the right track when she protested that the two reminiscing old warriors had only been *babies*. "But you'll pretend that you were men instead of babies," she added with passion, "and you'll be played in the movie by Frank Sinatra and John Wayne, or some of those other glamorous, war-loving dirty old men."

Vonnegut later subtitled his book *The Children's Crusade* as a result. And it turned out to be a highly unusual sort of novel, part science fiction, with the Dresden experience seen through the eyes of Billy Pilgrim, an ineffectual wartime chaplain's assistant. Billy has "come unstuck in time", after suffering brain damage in an air crash long after the war. He travels uncontrollably back and forth to different episodes in his life - visiting also the planet 'Tralfamadore" - thus allowing the full horror of the bombing of the city to be implied in perhaps the only way that was possible, since there was nothing of an imaginative kind that could be said about such a massacre.

I have only one small quibble. Towards the end Vonnegut makes references to a book called *The Destruction of Dresden,* quoting from a foreword various statistics and other thoughts about the raid. Among the statistics is a figure of 135,000 dead. Vonnegut has mentioned the figure elsewhere and seems to have used the book as a factual source. I have seen much lower figures from other sources, and also different accounts of the mix of people who happened to be in the city. I'm not suggesting that these different facts and figures make the raid more acceptable. The city was defenceless. Nor do I have any idea who was right. But in a 25th anniversary special edition of the novel the source was left to stand without comment. And the author of *The Destruction of Dresden* - and I'm not of course pretending to be the first to draw attention to this - was the controversial historian David Irving.

No writer is ever quite what he seems. Not even Kurt Vonnegut.

*

I did see him once. I attended a talk by him at the Cheltenham Literature Festival, in 1993. It was a long drive, from my home in Cheshire, and I'm not sure what I expected to get out of it.

Perhaps he would sign a copy of *Galapagos* for me at the book signing. Perhaps there would be the chance of a chat, for I had written to him a couple of times by now. He had replied, too, which rather surprised me, since he had said in print that he had given up replying to readers' letters because he invariably found that he had yet another new pen pal.

I'd sent him a copy of my *Guardian* piece, but my real purpose in writing had been in the hope of getting a good quote from him for my Saroyan books - guessing that he too would have been a fan in his younger days. This turned out to be true. They had also met once, at his home. This would have been sometime in the '70s. His second wife, the photographer Jill Kramentz, was putting together a computer file of well-known writers, and Saroyan had evidently been invited to have his photograph taken. In his letter, Vonnegut described him as somewhat tongue-tied.

I thought about this. Perhaps Saroyan felt shy or uncomfortable in the presence of a writer who was then at the peak of a fame which even surpassed his own, more than thirty years earlier. He would have been well into his sixties, too, while Vonnegut, although not young, was a good deal younger than he was. (In fact there was an age difference of fourteen years.) He no longer bore much resemblance to the hungry young writer his ex-wife (who wrote about her marriages to Saroyan and Walter Matthau in her 1992 memoir *Among the Porcupines*) remembered at the time of their first meeting - like Al Pacino in *The Godfather*. He had grown fat. But the chief reason why Saroyan felt uncomfortable around Vonnegut could simply have been their relative heights. He was short - no more than five-feet-six or seven - and in so far as he never mentioned this anywhere in his writings, it seems likely that it embarrassed him. Kurt Vonnegut stood *six-feet-three*.

I got the quote I wanted from Vonnegut ("William Saroyan's stories knocked my hat off when they first appeared "), but that didn't mean he would know who I was if I attempted to speak to him at the Festival. But then again he just *might*. I bought another copy of *Galapagos* in the bookshop, for possible signing later, then joined the people filing into the marquee for his talk.

The lady who introduced him quoted Graham Greene, who had described him as "one of the best living American writers". She thought it ought to be simply "the best". His talk was about an earlier generation of American literary figures, notably Hemingway and Fitzgerald - off the top of his head, as far as I could make out. I waited, and not altogether to my surprise he mentioned Saroyan at one point.

He paused, too, perhaps to check if anybody knew the name. It was a strange moment for me. My letters could have given him the idea that Saroyan was still well-remembered in England. If one person knew who he was, there should be others. I glanced about me but couldn't see any recognition of the name in the faces of the audience members I was sitting amongst, and the moment passed. Maybe I ought to have *waved*.

Afterwards I hoped to see him signing books and wondered if I'd have the courage to try to exchange a few words. There was nothing to show where this might happen, however. Then I saw a huddle of people, and a little commotion going on, but kept my distance. Next morning I read in the *Guardian* that he hadn't been up to book signings and had in fact cancelled a second talk scheduled for later in the week. Very odd. He had certainly seemed relaxed enough on the platform.

A few months later I sent him a copy of my new *Saroyan: Memoirs* anthology, with the request that he might be kind enough to pass it on to a publisher over there, adding that I wouldn't trouble him further. He described the material as only "so-so", but did say that my introduction was "good". It made it all seem worthwhile for a moment. And he *was* kind enough to do as I had requested. The small publishers were called Seven Stories Press (publishers later of his own little book *God Bless You Dr. Kevorkian*). They had never heard of Saroyan, and weren't interested. I kept my word and left him alone after that.

*

To my knowledge, information about the *real* Kurt Vonnegut has yet to emerge, so I can't comment on that. One has the feeling that he was a deeply sad, even damaged, soul - probably as a result of the Dresden experience and a loss of faith in humanity, in combination with certain tragedies in his own family life - notably the suicide of his mother, which happened around the same time, and the early death from cancer of his sister. Mark Vonnegut, however, in the introduction to a posthumous collection of unpublished writings, *Armageddon in Retrospect,* remembers his father more as a natural, friendly extrovert who appeared only to *want* to be the screwed-up character everybody thought he *was*. "An optimist posing as a pessimist," he suggests. He downplays an apparent suicide attempt in the 1980s. Commenting on his father's tremendous success as a writer - now taken for granted - he reminds us that for a very long time it looked as if such a thing could never possibly happen. *Slaughterhouse-5* wasn't published until he was *forty-six*.

I heard that Kurt Vonnegut had died on Friday, 13th April, 2007. In fact it had happened two days earlier, evidently as a result of brain injury sustained in a fall. In a black joke in *A Man Without a Country* he had said he was planning to sue the manufacturers of

Pall Mall cigarettes because - contrary to their clear promise on the package, and in spite of having chain-smoked them since he was about twelve - their product had not only failed to kill him, it had permitted him to live on into the presidency of George W Bush!

So, having claimed his father, his sister, his brother and his first wife, cancer did not in the end get *him*.

8
TRYING TO READ JOHN IRVING

Being rather particular about the books and authors I read is something I suspect I share with other writers. I suppose the worry is that we feel we have something to protect and don't like to risk poisoning the wellspring by indiscriminate reading. Daft, of course! We also prefer to own books rather than to borrow them from friends or from a library, and can't bear to dispose of them. And the longer we keep them the more stubborn we become. Ultimately, I suspect, we would like them somehow to become an organic part of us.

You would think this hang-up - together with my habit of spending months reading everything the writer I happen currently to be into has ever written, without a break - would have led more often than it has to reader's block. How did I ever in the end move on? Well, there may be a clue in the books on my shelves. I can see connections. One writer I already knew may have said something complimentary about another in a jacket quote, say, and there's nothing like having a novel or author recommended by someone you can trust. It can save a lot of scanning of the bookshop shelves. I do know for a fact, too, that a writer I was led to in this way was John Irving, Kurt Vonnegut's one-time creative-writing student and a novelist he seemed to champion almost from the moment the class broke up. I had more or less made up my mind to have him as my next literary hero before I had even dipped into him.

I'm aware that John Irving has been prolific, but I haven't exactly been keeping up with his output so I hesitate to say that his most famous novel today is *The World According to Garp*. It *used* to be, I think, and for once it was this well-known novel I tried first. I didn't finish it, however. The writing struck me as surprisingly ordinary, for one thing, though I was willing to persist. What I didn't know is that the novel is booby-trapped, to use a favourite Vonnegut expression. About half way through it, there is a moment - a horrific accident - which is so grotesquely awful, and at the same time so cunningly planned and choreographed, that I had to snap the book shut, never to reopen it. When I say that one character has his penis bitten off, and that it isn't even the *worst* thing that happens in that awful moment, it will give you an idea of what I'm talking about.

I left John Irving alone for a long time after that. The awful reality of the world as it sometimes intruded into one's life was quite enough for me. Invented horrors I could do without. As for serving them up in a way calculated to maximise the impact on the reader, that struck me as plain sick. And I still feel that way. In fact it's got worse with age. By all means conclude that I have lived too sheltered a life.

*

But I did notice in jacket quotes on his books that Vonnegut appeared to admire Irving more and more. As time passed I began to think I had been silly to react as strongly as I had, and decided to try the man again. If Kurt Vonnegut was a fan, that ought to be enough. I tend to go for slim books, too, and thought that safer. Irving's novels seemed to be mostly fat, but I found a thinnish early novel called *The 158-Pound Marriage* and decided on that for my next attempt, encouraged - though I was becoming wary - by a Vonnegut quote on the front cover: 'The most important American humorist to appear in the last ten years."

I managed to finish the book this time, though I'm sorry to say that I didn't laugh once. It had its awful moments, too, and seemed pretty unpleasant to me throughout. It's mostly about a *menage-à-quatre*. At first you imagine it's a wholesome arrangement, but inevitably it turns out to be no such thing. One of the characters is a wrestler - a sport Irving himself has been involved with - and a wrestling mat features frequently, in the sex scenes. Hardly mentioned are the young children of the two couples until, late on, they are all in a bath together when a rickety glass cabinet falls to pieces above them. This time, thankfully, no one is hurt and I didn't have to close the book, though I could imagine the author's temptation.

Maybe his short stories would be more palatable, I thought. I prefer short stories to most novels. So, only a little daunted, I next tried *Trying to Save Piggy Snead*, a collection of them. I found the book rather more to my liking. More intriguing, however, was an essay on Charles Dickens, at the end of the book. In it I found these words:

…It was his aim not to turn the stomach but to move the heart. But it is my strong suspicion that in a contemporary world, where hearts are more hardened, Dickens would have been motivated to turn the stomach, too, as the one way remaining for reaching those hardened hearts.

So there you have it. John Irving is writing for the hard-hearted. To read him you need a strong stomach. If like me, though, you are made of weaker stuff - or if you happen to have had some exposure to the real horrors of this world - I fancy his novels are best avoided. Any one of them could be booby-trapped and might blow up in your face. Sensitive souls might not like that.

Even so I have since tried another, after a further long gap, *Setting Free the Bears*. It's described by Vonnegut as "the most nourishing and satisfying novel I have read in years". Who could resist that? So I took it on holiday with me. Once again I didn't have to shut the book, but I found a further and unexpected obstacle: the writing this time was too good. His new books keep on piling up on the shelves - fat volume after fat volume - but *Setting Free the Bears* was another early work, written back in the 1960s, when the author was influenced by the Beat Generation writers, I fancy. It would be surprising if he wasn't. Here, the two main characters are on a motor bike trip:

…He wrenched down the headlight and slanted the beam to the river, but there wasn't any river. He pressed the kill button on the engine and we heard a river - we heard the wind making the bridge planks groan - and we felt how the bridge rails were damp from a rising spray. But in the light's beam there was only a gorge, falling into darkness; and the tilted firs, holding to the gorge walls, reached for help and didn't dare look down…

For page after page nothing much happens, and you smile only rarely, yet the sentences are amazing. In the end, though, this stuff can be tiring to read. It's a kind of poetry, really, and wonderful as it seems, you don't necessarily want pages and pages of it, what with life being so short and everything. Volumes of poetry are usually much slimmer than novels.

Maybe such prose is for younger minds than mine. I like clarity and simplicity these days. I brought *Setting Free the Bears* back from holiday unfinished, and I'm sorry to say that I rather avoided picking it up again, Kurt Vonnegut's strong recommendation notwithstanding.

9

EVELYN WAUGH AND THE TWITCH UPON THE THREAD

I reread one or two of his books from time to time, but the Evelyn Waugh period in my reading life was really in the 1970s. He occupied me almost exclusively from around 1976 to '79, with a resurgence of interest at the time of the television serialisation of *Brideshead Revisited* in the early '80s. Today he is well represented on the shelves of the bigger Waterstone's branches - though for some reason *The Ordeal of Gilbert Pinfold*, his most interesting book in my view, is usually missing. I'm sure he's still much read, as well. In fact there appears to be something of a Waugh industry still in existence forty years after his death, with his professional admirers and posthumous representatives occasionally unearthing and disseminating material which has long been out of sight or forgotten.

Two interesting memoranda by Evelyn Waugh were published in The *Guardian Saturday Review* several years ago, for example, in which he gave instructions to the Hollywood movie people in the late 1940s for the possible filming of certain scenes in *Brideshead Revisited*. Written during the war, the novel had been a big hit in America, but some doubt was cast in the editorial comment accompanying the pieces as to whether he was altogether serious about the film project, the thought being that he may have been simply enjoying a trip to California at someone else's expense during the British post-war austerity years.

Malcolm Muggeridge (in the I 960s) described Waugh as "probably the most accomplished writer today in the English language". I certainly had a similar admiration for him when I was reading his books some years later. Besides *Pinfold* - an autobiographical, self-revealing novel inspired by the mysterious voices he heard on a cruise when under the influence of alcohol and medication - I certainly loved *Scoop, The Loved One*, his *Sword of Honour* trilogy of wartime novels, and his collection of travel writings *When the Going was Good* - all rather better known. But, with Muggeridge, I have never much cared for his best-known novel of all. True, Granada Television made a wonderful job of the serialisation of *Brideshead,* but I rather feel that viewers were more seduced by the production values than the story. Waugh was a snob and a Catholic convert, and those aspects of the man, always lurking in his books, are most in evidence in this novel. For me, a non-Catholic - close to being an outright atheist, in fact - there is a kind of sickness running through the whole thing.

Most unpleasant - for me, I stress - is the return to his ancestral home of the dying Lord Marchmain. He has lived the life of a reprobate abroad, mainly in Venice, for many years, and his denial of his faith has remained intact. Now it is to be tested in the severest way.

*

In the first of his memoranda, Waugh explains to the film people what this episode is about: "The Roman Catholic church has the unique power of keeping remote control on human souls which have once been part of her. GK Chesterton has compared this power to the fisherman's line, which allows the fish the illusion of free play in the water, and yet has him by the hook. In his own time the fisherman, by a 'twitch upon the thread' draws, the fish to land."

That is the fate of poor Lord Marchmain on his deathbed. The priest and others watch carefully for a signal, however slight and unwilling, as death approaches. And sure enough the dying man, in his extremity, at last weakens and recants, leaving those at the bedside much relieved and thankful. Waugh describes this process as "the operation of Grace; the unmerited and unilateral act of love by which God continually calls souls to himself'.

For my part I have to say that I find all this pretty repugnant. Others may feel differently, and I respect that. One thing I have noticed, though, is that religious people, of whatever persuasion, when challenged, often insist that, faced with death, the unbeliever will find himself crying out to God for mercy.

Does that in fact happen? Zealots like to cite the case of soldiers dying on the battlefield. I have thankfully never been in such a terrible situation, so I wouldn't know about that.

But I read in the paper a little while before the Waugh memoranda appeared an uplifting account by a lapsed Catholic who had been close to death - and had *expected* to die - but had survived against the odds. He said he had been fearful that when the moment came he would not have the strength to hold out. But to his great surprise and relief he had come through the ordeal without recanting. Of course he hadn't *actually* died, but that to me is a heartening story. It must be so much harder for a Catholic.

But then what do I know? Well, it happens that I have been within hailing distance of the edge myself. I mean I have known what it is like to expect to die. It happened twelve years ago. I had a total stomach blockage, which it was believed could only be cancer. Even after an exploratory operation my surgeon couldn't be sure that the abdominal "mass" he had found, pressing against the intestine, wasn't malignant. It took time to establish that it wasn't. I also had the most extraordinary hallucinations while recovering on the ward. I don't recall thinking about God at any point through it all, however. But then ours wasn't a religious home, so I hadn't had religion planted in me at an early, impressionable, *trusting* age.

Not long afterwards my wife went a step further and died - from leukaemia. She *was* a believer, though not a Catholic. I truly hope she is now in heaven, and for that to happen I don't believe that any thread twitching would have been necessary. What an unpleasant idea!

10

THE SAD END OF MALCOLM MUGGERIDGE

"Gibberidge" my late wife called him, and looking back it seems pretty apt. A reactionary writer and sage whose years of greatest fame were in the Swinging Sixties, Malcolm Muggeridge had a wonderful command of language, whether writing or speaking, but he was out of tune with his times and often misunderstood. He is better remembered now, I fancy, for his contorted vowels and facial expressions, once mimicked so beautifully on television by Mike Yarwood, than for his way with words. Television was a medium Muggeridge himself claimed to loathe, but seemed unable to stay away from.

As an example of how difficult it was to communicate reactionary opinions at that time, I remember seeing him on television addressing an audience of students at a Scottish university. (I think he was rector at the time.) There was a proposal that they be given free contraceptive pills, then quite a new thing. It was a development that Mr Muggeridge was very definitely against, but one of the young persons accused him of not making himself clear.

"I view the suggestion with the utmost abhorrence," he explained, enunciating each syllable with precision. "Is that clear enough for you?"

But the student continued to look puzzled.

His extraordinary charisma was the problem. Everyone was eager to know what he thought, but his answers tended to fall on deaf ears. On another TV occasion he took questions from a studio audience alongside Bernard Levin, also a famous pundit of the day. It was embarrassing. No one asked Levin a single question. Muggeridge, striving as ever to keep his ego in check, took no apparent pleasure in the situation. Nor did his opinions cause outrage. The audience listened politely, and as usual not very attentively, I suspect.

Here is Bernard Levin himself on the man:

What a piece of work is Mr Muggeridge! Who knows him loves him; who meets him bathes in the glow he radiates; who talks to him reveres. How can this be the same man as *the harsh Savonarola of the telly, calling others to righteousness in the name of* a *man, or god, who insisted that only those without sin should cast the stones.*

That's from a review of his marvellous two-volume autobiography, *Chronicles* of *Wasted Time,* and he was certainly a sinner. There were intended to be three volumes, but the third was never finished. He was born in 1903, and the book takes his life as far as the end of World War II, covering an early spell in colonial India, life as a Fleet Street hack, and his wartime adventures in the Secret Service. But the most fascinating part for me is his account of his time in Soviet Russia in the early '30s. He had married into the family of the socialist icon Beatrice Webb, who with her husband Sidney would soon publish their monumental folly, *Soviet Communism: a New Civilisation.* Muggeridge and his wife Kitty, rose-tinted spectacles firmly in place, left an England languishing in the misery of a terrible depression for which no one had a credible answer to embrace this new civilisation - never, as they thought, to return.

Bertrand Russell at the Free Trade Hall

It was his gradual realisation that the Soviet regime, Stalin at the helm, was in fact well-advanced in setting up one of the most monstrous tyrannies in history, which later resulted in Muggeridge's great distrust of all progressive ideas. He looked on in astonishment and dismay at the imbecile credulity of his visiting socialist heroes, as they were escorted around the model farms and factories and fed entirely bogus statistics and ludicrous accounts of happy, well-fed workers and peasants in a land of plenty. When he tried to alert his colleagues on the *Manchester Guardian* to the deception his reports were not believed. And there was also the censorship to cope with. One comment that did escape their attention, tagged on to some nonsense about the latest five-year plan, was: "Suggest tell marines!"

*

Malcolm Muggeridge didn't publish very many books. His primary output was as a journalist. After the two volumes of *Chronicles of Wasted Time*, my favourites were (and are) *Tread Softly, for You Tread on My Jokes*, an elegant collection of his best essays, and *The Thirties*, his hilarious account of the cheerless decade which preceded World War II. Also enjoyable is Richard Ingrams' *God's Apology*, an account of Muggeridge's friendship in middle life with Hugh Kingsmill and Hesketh Pearson. From Kingsmill he picked up the useful term "Dawnism", to describe an unwarranted belief in the power for good of progressive ideas.

Scripts from his many television programmes, along with other TV and radio interviews, debates and general punditry, were collected in *Muggeridge Through the Microphone* (1966). It was later expanded to become *Muggeridge Ancient and Modern*, as a tie-in for a programme in which he commented, with some distaste, on his younger performing self. There are interesting interviews with

Lord Reith, Leonard Woolf and PG Wodehouse (to whose aid he came at the end of the war, following the trouble caused by Wodehouse's light-hearted broadcasts from Nazi Germany while briefly a prisoner), and a discussion on the meaning of *Pilgrim's Progress* with Aneurin Bevan (who saw it as an early socialist polemic). But I was most intrigued (as might be expected) by a radio debate with Bertrand Russell in 1957.

Russell never commented on the programme - entitled, "Is the Nature of Progress an Illusion" - in *his* writings, but Muggeridge certainly remembered it. I was only eighteen at the time, so I missed the actual broadcast (I wouldn't then have heard of either of them), but it appears that Russell lost his temper. In his 1995 biography, Richard Ingrams (who wrongly describes it as a TV debate) relates how "the great philosopher became almost apoplectic with rage when Muggeridge challenged his view that Christianity had caused most of the world's troubles". This doesn't come out quite so straightforwardly in the debate as it appears in print, however. Russell does attack Christianity, but he also lets it be known that he regards *all* religions as horrible, and wishes that *none* of them had ever existed.

Their general difference of opinion is about whether human life can keep on getting better. Russell argues passionately that we should try to alleviate suffering and increase happiness. With equal passion, Muggeridge expresses the opinion that while we may make material improvements to our lives, that doesn't alter its essential character. Efforts simply to improve the lot of mankind can be counter-productive, as in Soviet Russia and Nazi Germany, both of which were driven by material rather than spiritual values. Russell says that both were in fact inculcating a new religion, and new religions are even worse than the old ones.

The only thing that any human being could possibly achieve is simply to be good, Muggeridge insists. This strikes Russell as priggish.

Who was right? I would say that life is now less cruel than it once was, at least in the democracies, and that counts for a lot in my book. But then, with the disaster of the euro, we may be moving back to the kind of turbulence in Europe with which my own life began. Perhaps man really *is* born to trouble, with no escape.

As for Russell's loss of temper, well, I'm sure it happened. In *Russell Remembered* (1 970), his friend Rupert Crawshay-Williams describes how he was easy to wind up, and was apt in private to express his opinions on issues he felt very strongly about in extreme form, a tendency which could sometimes spill over into his public utterances. (I remember how he once described political leaders of the day, like Macmillan, as "wickeder than Hitler", because of the probable end result of their nuclear policies.) He was also growing deaf in old age, and this evidently made him worse.

Their respective ages in the debate is something that shouldn't in fact be overlooked, though neither Muggeridge himself nor his biographer refers to it. Muggeridge was a highly intelligent and incisive interviewer, then aged fifty-three and at the height of his powers. Russell by contrast was close to eighty-five.

But why were the two men so very different in their views? Maybe their upbringing was a factor. Muggeridge described his early years in "A Socialist Childhood" (one of the television scripts in *Muggeridge Through the Microphone).* His father was steeped in socialism, and was briefly a Labour MP. While he loved the man and didn't want to disappointment him, it was perhaps inevitable that he would be drawn to a different set of values and beliefs. There was also a strong radical tradition in Russell's aristocratic family, but this was mixed with a puritanical element. There were cold baths and morning prayers at Pembroke Lodge, with no food treats for children. He loved his grandmother, but she only allowed herself to sit in an armchair in the evenings. He had to conceal his developing radical opinions from the grown-ups in whose midst he lived (he was the only child in the house, or the whole neighbourhood) by writing them down in code, using Greek letters, and wasn't able to speak his mind at all freely until he escaped to Cambridge.

Muggeridge also went to Cambridge, though their attitudes and experiences could hardly have been more different. While for Russell it was a liberation and he made lifelong friends from the start, Muggeridge was there to fulfil his *father's* ambition. He studied the Natural Science Tripos (chemistry, physics and zoology) and while he managed to scrape a pass, thereafter he never gave the subjects a moment's thought. He was no scientist. As he wrote in his autobiography:

From the very beginning of my life I never doubted that words were my métier. There was nothing else I ever wanted to do except use them; no other accomplishment or achievement I ever had the slightest regard for or desire to emulate. I have always loved words and still love them, for their own sake. For the power and beauty of them; for the wonderful things that can be done with them.

About the only subject he and Russell could have agreed on was Soviet Russia. Alone among the British intelligentsia, Russell had spoken out against the developing tyranny after a visit there (which included a talk with Lenin) as early as 1920. Muggeridge praises the stand he took in *Tread Softly, for You Tread on My Jokes*. He only came to recognise what was going on himself more than a decade later.

*

Although my general feelings were closer to Russell's, I used to be quite a Muggeridge fan, much to the puzzlement of my socialist friends. I wrote to him a couple of times, and had one reply (now lost). That would have been in the '60s, and I expect I questioned his reactionary opinions on the social issues of the time. I mentioned Russell, too, for he described him as "not a good guide in moral matters", I remember. In later life even Russell himself came to question his own earlier views on marriage, as expressed in *Marriage and Morals*.

Long afterwards, when I was writing to as many prominent people as I could think off who might provide me with a quote to help with my campaign to revive William Saroyan's writings - and it's hard to imagine anyone less likely than Malcolm Muggeridge - I sent him a copy of a story of Saroyan's that I thought might just interest him. It was written In Moscow in 1935, while Saroyan was on a tour of Europe following the success of his first book, *The Daring Young Man on the Flying Trapeze*. The story (like much of Saroyan's early work it's part story, part memoir and part essay) ends with an imaginary conversation with a cynical, laughing little street dog, hanging around by the river. The narrator is trying to think well of Russia and the communist experiment, but the little dog shoots down his every positive thought. ("No more fear," I said. "Ha ha," said the little dog. "Not much, comrade, not much.") It didn't really surprise me that there was no response to my approach. They were such different writers, and Muggeridge by this time was after all in his eighties.

*

Unlike, say, John Betjeman, or more recently Alan Bennett, he never did attain the position of a National Treasure. He didn't come across in his *N* or other public appearances as cuddly exactly. Those who met him may have bathed in the glow he radiated, but to television viewers he didn't appear all that "comfortable in his skin", as they say these days. In fact in later life Malcolm Muggeridge turned increasingly - and as it seemed rather desperately - to religion. It was a process which aroused a good deal of public cynicism. although it wasn't really a new departure for him. Anyone who can find a copy of his 1930s book *In a Valley of this Restless Mind* will see that his religious impulses were well-developed when he was still a comparatively young man.

During these last years I waited impatiently for the third volume of his autobiography to appear. But as he entered old age his name was seen less frequently in print, while his television appearances also dried up. There was a confrontation with John Cleese and company over the *Monty Python's Life of Brian* film, which some saw as embarrassing. Soon afterwards he was shown being accepted into the Catholic Church, a move which many thought long overdue. After that it was public silence, more or less, until his death in 1990. Five years later, in the final chapter of his biography, Richard Ingrams briefly told the sad truth of his final years of decline.

Malcolm Muggeridge had had a tendency to comment unkindly on the ageing process in others, while viewing the prospect of his own decline and demise in a more romantic light.

But as the end of his life approached he became less serene and increasingly senile, it appears, the final circumstances turning out to be anything but romantic. He had frequently expressed a distaste for the wonders of modern medicine, too, which added to the poignancy of the situation.

Following a minor stroke, accompanied by his wife he was moved from a rest home into hospital, where a seemingly bizarre decision was taken that both needed hip-replacement operations. She was to recover. He died struggling to regain control of his movements in a rehabilitation centre.

11
SAMUEL BUTLER REVISITED

I used to meet with retired friends for a pub lunch and chat once a week, when we would wrestle with some pretty deep issues. You need leisure in your life for that. One time, I remember, we were discussing whether it was essential for a society to have a set of moral rules to live by - with a religious or cultural foundation - or if people could get along well enough without. Our debates were apt to be a bit competitive. It can be useful in such circumstances to be able to introduce something the others aren't ready for and can't so easily dismiss, and I was able to quote the Victorian writer Samuel Butler - or more accurately an essay by Bertrand Russell in which he mentions Samuel Butler.

The quote (which I will return to later) didn't win the argument for me exactly - nothing ever did - but it made me look for Samual Butler's books when I was next in Waterstone's. I was very surprised not to be able to find anything. Could *The Way of All Flesh* and *Erewhon* really be forgotten now? They had certainly stayed in my mind, over several decades. If set me searching through my store of accumulated ancient paperbacks at home. I emerged after a struggle with a Premier World Classics edition of *The Way of All Flesh* only, published in 1960. I dare say I could still have *Erewhon* somewhere, though probably not the less famous *Erewhon Revisited*. I don't believe I ever read that book. In fact I suspect I only know of its existence via Bertrand Russell.

The reputation *The Way of All Flesh* once had was evident from the copious cover notes on the old copy I'd unearthed. Samuel Butler was "the *enfant terrible* of literature. No writer ever assaulted the morality and traditions of his age with more furious dedication or pitiless contempt than this lonely genius." The age of course was the Victorian one, and the book was thought so daring that it could be published only after his death (in 1902), "bold as Samuel Butler was". Called "a diabolical novel" by its critics and detractors, it "stormed the ramparts of Victorian complacency and stripped bare its suffocating tyranny over the social, educational and religious institutions of the day". Phew!

My own feelings about *The Way of All Flesh* never somehow quite matched what I had been led to expect, but I had read the novel in the right spirit long ago. I wanted to believe what it said on the cover. But the main character, Ernest Pontifex, had struck me as more than a little wet.

His early mission in life was to save souls, and there is a scene where he is earnestly trying to persuade a prostitute to abandon her immoral ways when his secret hero, a handsome, athletic young fellow called Townley, comes bounding up the stairs with other business in mind. Poor innocent Ernest can only slink miserably away. But I couldn't quarrel with the basic idea that the moral education being instilled into young Victorians was hardly preparing them for real life as they must one day encounter it.

The book was admired by writers as diverse as DH Lawrence and EM Forster, while George Bernard Shaw "never ceased to proclaim himself Butler's disciple". My personal view of *The Way of All Flesh* would I'm sure have remained respectful, if slightly puzzled, had I not later read a piece on Butler and his novel by Malcolm Muggeridge, who had once written a biography of the man.

Muggeridge had reached the conclusion from his researches that Butler "had stumbled upon the moral landscape ahead when he thought he was prudently adjusting himself to the existing one. No one could have been more queasily conservative, more timid, conformist and respectable, than he was." His chief complaint in life was against his father, Canon Butler, who was reluctant to support him and thought he ought to earn a living, since his books made no money. 'The Canon's greatest offence in his son's eyes was to go on living, thereby delaying the blessed moment when Butler would inherit. His letters asking for news of his father's health were about as tenderly phrased as income tax demands." On balance Muggeridge thought *The Way of All Flesh* "about the most ignoble book ever written".

But one thing in his essay intrigues me. Samuel Butler was evidently homosexual. Ernest Pontifex was essentially Butler himself, while Townley was based on Pauli, an impecunious young man he worshipped and with whom he had his longest and most expensive affair. Yet Muggeridge has much fun describing Butler's visits with Festing Jones - his first biographer and also homosexual, one gathers - to a certain French lady on Handel Street. She dealt with their "immediate exigencies", leaving them free to lavish their "romantic ecstasies" on Pauli. Was that normal behaviour for homosexuals at that time?

Erewhon was perhaps a more interesting book. The hero, a man called Higgs, discovers a remote country where Victorian notions of morality are turned on their heads. Anyone afflicted with the distressing illness of kleptomania receives enormous sympathy, for instance, while a sufferer from tuberculosis has to keep the fact concealed or risk social disgrace.

*

Bertrand Russell mentions *Erewhon Revisited* in his essay "Why I am Not a Christian". I told my friends that in *Erewhon* Higgs had escaped from the remote country in a balloon. Russell describes how on his return in the sequel, ten years later, he finds himself worshipped as the Sun King, with the Feast of the Ascension about to be celebrated. He is indignant and goes up to the high priests of the new religion, Professors Hanky and Panky, threatening to expose all this for the nonsense it is. But he is told that the morals and laws of the country are now bound up in this myth, and if the people once discover that the Sun King was in reality only the man Higgs they will all become wicked.

12
JACK TREVOR STORY: AN UNAUTHORISED BIOGRAPHY

Writers can be quickly forgotten. Or it can happen slowly. In the case of Jack Trevor Story's literary hero and mentor, William Saroyan - though they never met, nor even exchanged letters - it has been slow, starting before he was forty and continuing (at least in America) down to the present day, thirty years after his death at seventy-two. In Jack's case - although he died twenty years ago as I write, to the month - it is taking rather less time. The process may even be complete, or as complete as being forgotten ever gets for a writer who has been at all well-known.

It can't be an absolute. What I tend to mean these days is that you no longer see their books on the shelves in Waterstone's, and Jack's books disappeared from them some time in the '90s. A paperback of his trilogy of Albert Argyle novels *(Live Now, Pay Later* etc) hung around for a while after his death, but hangs around no longer. They were good, but those who load the shelves at Waterstone's are pretty ruthless. You certainly won't find a copy of my biography of Story, *Romantic Egotist*, lingering unnoticed there or anywhere else now. It found its way into precious few bookshops even when fresh (as will be seen).

I discovered that Jack was a Saroyan fan one Saturday morning in the early '70s, when he published a long article on our mutual hero in the *Guardian*, revealing the great influence the American-Armenian writer had had on his early career in particular. It was quite a moment for me, for I had until then imagined myself to be Saroyan's last British fan. Besides his longer pieces, Jack had a cult column in the paper, but I hadn't been paying it any attention. I thought now of writing to him, and continued to think of that for six or seven years - until I was busy compiling my anthology of Saroyan's best writings that would eventually become *The New Saroyan Reader*. Then, by coincidence, a letter from Jack appeared one day in the newspaper's correspondence columns, accompanied by an address: *Stacey Hill Farm, Wolverton, Milton Keynes, Bucks*. I had had the vague idea for a little while that if I could find a famous name who was willing to co-edit the book it would help it into print. Why not Jack Trevor Story? So I wrote to him, expecting only a scribbled note in return - if that.

But he replied at some length - almost as if I was a long lost friend! He took me for a Jack Trevor Story *fan*, of course, and mentioned a new story of his in the latest issue of *Punch*. I raced down to my newsagents (l was then only thirty-nine) and bought a copy. On the rare occasions when I had casually tried to read his stuff in the *Guardian* I had found him difficult. Now, with more of a motive, I expected that to change. found, though, that I couldn't make head or tail of the *Punch* story.

I managed to say *something* about it, however, in my next letter, before pulling him back to the reason for my first approach. He was far too busy to get involved, he told me, for I had caught him in the middle of filming a new television series, *Jack on the Box*. It was to be screened in six episodes at peak time on ITV. But he stayed in touch, continuing to write surprisingly long letters for someone so busy. I had become one of his regular correspondents. I didn't know then that he was a compulsive letter writer, willing to exchange letters with just about anyone who would keep up their end. Although filming was well advanced, he was hoping to include an interview with William

Saroyan in Jack *on the Box*, and I was able to help him out with Saroyan's Paris address: *74 Rue Taitbout*. Sad to say, the interview never happened. Saroyan would by then have been too old and deaf and difficult, I suspect, as well as too ill.

So that's how well-known Jack Trevor Story himself once was, back in 1979 - a prime-time show on ITV! Surprisingly, though, it turned out also to be the moment when his career began to nosedive. Not that *Jack on the Box* was badly received. There were excellent reviews in the papers, many of them with photographs. It just so happened that we were in the middle of the "Winter of Discontent", and when only two episodes had been shown it became a victim of the first technicians' strike in television history. The remainder were screened about a year later - after midnight, as I recall. The publishers of a tie-in book and reprints of several of Jack's novels went bust.

*

Yet in spite of this set-back, we remained close pen friends. In fact as life got harder for him, with publishers no longer very willing to take on his new books - which seemed ironic, as I was just starting to get into them myself - and with his young soul-mate wife having at some point walked out, his letters became more frequent.

He had been living for some time in a rambling flat spread over the top floor of an old farmhouse, having moved to the Milton Keynes area from a shared flat in Hampstead to take up the unusual position of Writer in Residence for the new city. (Liz Leyh, creator of Milton Keynes' famous concrete cows, was the *Sculptor* in Residence.) But the post had been for a year only, and by the mid '80s, far away from the London scene, he was becoming trapped and isolated. One afternoon when I was in the area I called in to see him without prior notice. I found him hard at work on a piece for *Punch* that Alan Coren had commissioned, for which he would be paid £50, he told me. Alongside his ancient Adler typewriter, sitting on a small card table, were a few coins which he said was all the money he had in the world. I took him out for a meal.

Calling in became something of a regular thing, despite our living a hundred-and-fifty miles apart. My elder daughter was at university in the south and I had often to transport her stuff back and forth. The farm was close to my route - though with the bewildering Milton Keynes road system it was hard to find at first. Even members of his family had been known to turn back defeated when attempting a visit. This may well have added to his isolation. Sometimes we would drive up the A5 into Stony Stratford for a drink or to eat, though he had a curious aversion to lunch - picked up, I gathered, from a long association with film crews, who were obsessed with it.

Despite his penury, he hadn't been completely abandoned by the world, or by his family, I learned. He had a total of eight children, by two women. A wealthy photographer son, based in London, was paying his rent, while there were daughters living a little closer. Quite why he was being permitted to live on in the flat (the farmhouse had otherwise been converted into a museum), I never did find out. Jack himself now looked older and balder than he had in *Jack* on *the* Box, and a lot slimmer, too - due, I imagined, to his usually meagre diet. I remember thinking that if you wanted to lose weight, the best method was to be short of cash to buy food. He told me he had been known to live on porridge in really bad times. But the spacious flat was surprisingly clean and neat - as was Jack himself.

Working for a big company (ICI) that had been able to ride out a recession we'd now passed through, I was feeling prosperous and found his situation hard to comprehend. A writer with a famous name would surely soon bounce back, I thought. To be in such a situation was the dream of every wannabe writer. This was the author of *The Trouble with Harry* (filmed by Hitchcock, no less), *Live Now, Pay Later* (also filmed),/ *Sit in Hanger Lane*, *One Last Mad Embrace*, *Little Dog's Day*, *The Wind in the Snottygobble Tree* and countless other novels, film and television scripts, broadcast short stories, and journalistic pieces of every kind. But the truth was that Jack (born in 1917) was now in his seventies. The decline in his fortunes would sadly be permanent.

His later novels were rather wild, incidentally, though I had grown well used to his writing by this time. *Little Dog's Day* is probably the best - at least Auberon Waugh gave it one of his gold medals. Art Henry, who is recovering from a bizarre transplant operation in which he has been given a monkey's heart, wanders the streets playing his lonely trumpet in search of his lost poodle (Jack had a real poodle in his life). Everyone - his family, co-workers - is keeping well back, half expecting him to drop down dead at any moment. In fact they've already begun to divide his possessions - only for him to return inconveniently from the brink. But this world is normal enough. Only gradually does it become apparent that the characters are living in a nightmarish police state, with an underclass in the ghettos who are subjected to chemical experiments from the air, and from time to time selectively cemented over, or "Hitlerised", whenever their activities threaten the smooth running of the system…

It's hard to imagine anything more different from William Saroyan's popular and rather sentimental novel, *The Human Comedy!*

Another favourite of mine is *The Wind in the Snottygobble Tree*, in which the central character, a cowardly dreamer called Marchmont, bored with his job in a travel agents, begins to make little demands on its customers, such as to deliver a mysterious package to a Mr So-and so, at present holidaying in a certain hotel in some East European city. The contents of these packages are quite meaningless, but Marchmont finds himself drawn into the lethal game of international espionage. Terrifying happenings follow, including a plot to replace the Pope - scheduled to visit Britain - with a deluded inmate from a lunatic asylum. The real Pope is to be electrocuted via his chamber pot, as he relieves himself while journeying in his Popemobile… (The "snottygobble tree" of the title is a colloquial name for a species of yew in Jack Trevor Story's part of the world, it seems. Grown over refuse, and given plenty of humous and an occasional dressing of dry blood, it produces slimy berries the juice from which you can't get off your hands - poisonous, but good for you provided you don't eat them.)

*

My visits to Stacey Hill Farm continued for a year or two before the idea surfaced that I should write Jack's biography. Others might have taken on the job, although of course they would have been professionals who would have had carefully to weigh up if it would be worth their valuable time. Certainly there was no way he was ever going to do the job himself. Not straightforwardly. For Jack autobiography was art - his life something to mix into his fiction and journalism. In his own mind he had written the book several times already. So I began taking a tape recorder along on my visits. I couldn't see how I was ever going to be able to talk to many other people. He would have to be my primary source himself.

The early sessions - though at longish intervals - went well and the book was progressing nicely. I had covered his poverty-stricken single- parent boyhood in Burwell [in the Fens), his adolescence and young adulthood in Cambridge (he played guitar in a band and once won a *Melody Maker* prize), his career in industry (he became an electronics engineer, working for Marconi's), and his war years in which (unlike his father, who had been killed very late in the First World War) he was lucky to be in a reserved occupation, his early years as a professional writer (he was rather cheated by Hitchcock), his domestic difficulties in those years (the two women in his life lived in the same house at one point, where it seems they got along very well), his work as a successful film scriptwriter - in fact the biography was well advanced when, in the summer of 1990, Jack suddenly had a kind of nervous breakdown.

He had always been something of a manic-depressive, and for a time the manic side really got the upper hand. He was hospitalised for a spell, after which his family couldn't hold him. He escaped from one house and spent two nights sleeping rough (pretending to be a professor of botany from Leicester University), until a friend came to his rescue and drove him home to Milton Keynes. But then severe depression set in. I only found out about this months later. My book was completely stalled, meanwhile, and would probably have to be abandoned, I believed. In fact I seriously wondered if Jack would ever recover.

Luckily he did, and we started tentatively to meet again. But there had been a big change in his attitude. He was becoming concerned for the first time about his reputation - and not before time, you might say! I mean, who the hell was *I* to write his biography? We were as different as it was possible for two men to be - like chalk and cheese. In fact that was the title of my first chapter. Having by now read parts of it, he told me that my book was rubbish, insisting that if it was published at all it would have to be labelled "unauthorised". I said that that was bloody ridiculous, with all the help he'd given me. I came very close to giving up. He even said he suspected my motives - and at the same time a BBC radio producer was interviewing him for a programme which he also didn't like the idea of. He suspected *his* motives, too. (It would later be broadcast on Radio 4 as "Jack's Last Tape".) There was some kind of conspiracy going on, he seemed to think-which I suppose is understandable when you consider the plots of some of his novels.

But whenever it looked as if I might actually abandon the project a letter would drop on my doormat urging me to continue with it. I was also in touch with another penfriend of his, a Mrs Dunstall, known as "Floss" to her friends, who lived down in Kent. Floss was quite a lady. She had a son who was a musician, and she knew and met show-business people, notably Roger Moore. Jack was telling her in his letters that he was being difficult in the hope of improving the biography. She had been reading it chapter by chapter, however, and advised me to pay no attention to him. It would be a bestseller, she reckoned.

It was all rather bewildering, but somehow we limped on to a last taped interview, late in 1991, which gave me pretty much everything I needed for my concluding chapters. That was shortly after he'd had a serious fall down a flight of wooden steps at the farmhouse, banging his head on heavy plumbing. It had resulted in a further spell in hospital and had affected his health, he told me, in some undefined way. Even so, we parted on good terms that last time. He was always careful to ask about my family, all of whom had met him at one time or another.

Back home, however, I realised that I needed more information on a trip he'd made to California in the early '80s. In some trepidation, in my snug ICI office, I picked up the telephone. And that was when things did become pretty dramatic…

…Jack's mood turned to irritation when we had got through the pleasantries and he realised why I had called. I told him what I understood of the trip, which wasn't much. 'You know almost nothing about it, do you?" he said, in what sounded like amazement… But he consented to run quickly through the facts while I scribbled notes. Then he did turn nasty. Out came all his stored up *hatred of what I was doing: my motives, my refusal to consider major rewriting, my hopeless failure to recapture his golden Cambridge years, my deadness to his musical life (I was the only person he knew in whose presence he didn't play his guitar), and above all the sneer in everything I wrote, in my every utterance - my mocking tone, my obscene plan to end the book leaving him an isolated old has-been. I said I was perfectly ready to end the book on* a *positive note if I could. I would like nothing better. Then I got some of my own stuff in about all the time and effort I had expended and how he ought to be thankful he was dealing with someone of my integrity, who wasn't simply trying to use him. How I had several times, knowing how he felt, tried to abandon the project, only to be encouraged to carry on by none other than himself. And how disappointed I was by his attitude when I had hoped all along that my book might actually do him* a *bit of good, insulting as that must now*

sound. But I couldn't keep this up and began to stumble over my words, whereupon he did a mocking echo of this stumbling...

He hung up at that point, and there followed an uncharacteristic silence from him. I tried writing, but could get no response, which really was unusual. Once, after a similar row, he had written in a puzzled way: "I seem to have irritated you." I was beginning to worry, yet I wasn't ready for the call I had a week later from the writer Martin Seymour-Smith. I had been slow to get the news. He had been asked to write Jack Trevor Story's obituary for the next morning's *Times*, and needed help. Later, I was told that the body hadn't been discovered for two days.

*

This was a lot more shocking for me than William Saroyan's unexpected death ten years earlier (when I was in New York, hoping to find a publisher for my anthology), yet I was also excited to find that once again I seemed to be in the right place at the right time. There were big obituary notices in all the broadsheets (plus an appreciation by me in the *Guardian*), and even a less serious one in the *Daily Mail* (who telephoned me, hoping for something really salacious to include). Jack may have hated the book, but he surely would not have expected me at this late point to abandon the project. He was a professional. I felt I owed it to him to publish it - or to try to. Labelled "unauthorised", of course, as he had been insisting.

I was still in contact with Gerald Pollinger, and between us we tried a number of London publishers. I felt certain someone would take it on. Jack Trevor Story was still a fairly well-known name, if the obituary notices were anything to go by, glimpses of whose chaotic life had appeared in many newspaper and magazine articles over the years - not to mention on the television screen. I also had a different angle, in as much as I saw him as a misunderstood character.

You might, for example, think that the parents of the young girl he had married in his sixties would have chased down from their home in the north-east, bent upon to bringing her back. Instead, they moved down to Milton Keynes *themselves* and took up residence a few streets away from the farmhouse. Long after the girl had left him, Jack told me he was still pushing her father around in a wheelchair! That episode was far more typical of his real life than most people ever appreciated. I recall saying something critical on the phone about him myself once - to Philip Purser, a friend of his. He pulled me up short.

"Always remember that Jack is a very nice man!" he told me.

I thought it all made a fascinating story, and had every confidence in other respects that the book was pretty good - notwithstanding his own attitude to it. But once again the moment passed. Even with a prestigious agency behind me, there was nothing doing. Floss couldn't believe it. A year or more after his death I found myself with no option but to take the book to a "vanity" publisher, as they used to be called (it's now called self-publishing), if I was ever going to see it in print.

Yet despite this the *Guardian* ran a full-page linked piece by Byron Rogers, who described *Romantic Egotist* as a "little comic classic". Then Auberon Waugh (a very nice man) commissioned a review for the *Literary Review*, and Philip Purser wrote a long article for the *London Review of Books*. The *Manchester Evening News* did a nice review as well. But this was all to no avail, it has to be said, for the problem with vanity publishers is that there are never any books in the shops. Amazon might have been useful, but this was before the internet had really got established.

Sales of *Romantic Egotist* were just about sufficient for a second edition, even so, this time with quotes by George Melly, Sue Townsend and others on the back cover, along with a glowing one from Stephen Fry on the front: A *wonderful book about an extraordinary and deeply unusual writer and man.* I drove all over the place with it - also carrying photocopies of the reviews and obituary notices - visiting branches of Waterstone's. I spent a whole day as well trudging around the London bookshops. It was when Fry - rather less famous then than he is today, but still a big name -was in the headlines, after mysteriously walking out of a West End play by Simon Gray. Yet nobody anywhere would take a single copy.

Jack had a name-recognition problem. "Who *is* this Jack Trevor?" the man I spoke to in one of the big branches of Waterstone's asked me. That was the last straw. Someone running a bookshop was so lazy and stupid that he couldn't even read a name consisting of three words! It used to plague Jack himself. Letters would arrive for him almost every day addressed to 'Trevor Story", or "Jack Trevor-Storey", or some other irritating variant. "Jack Trevor" was the one, however, that *really* drove him mad.

But am I bitter about all this? Well, really no more bitter than Jack Trevor Story was when Alfred Hitchcock effectively stole *The Trouble with Harry* from him for £100.

*

As with William Saroyan, I accumulated a lot of correspondence and other material while I was working on Jack's biography, which ended up in my loft. How long do you keep such stuff? Again as with Saroyan, I used to believe that one day there would surely be a revival, and the material in this case included a copy of at least one complete book manuscript (entitled "My Life with Bing Crosby"), which he'd never been able to place. I can't now see there ever being a revival. I'm certainly not capable of creating one myself, and I doubt if anybody else is going to bother. So when I moved house in 2007 I dumped most of the stuff. I've kept all our letters, though. And the tapes. I expect I'll enjoy listening to *those* again one day.

RIP Jack Trevor Story.

13
HL MENCKEN AND THE GODS OF OLD

Here's a writer to hunt for in the second-hand bookshops now - or scour the internet. Mencken isn't forgotten, but his books are difficult to come by, so you may have to search pretty hard. I've been keeping an eye open for them myself for some years and all I've been able to find is an old Travellers' library edition of *Selected Prejudices: Second Series*.

But I had known all along that Mencken was a writer and critic of fearsome reputation. Quite a reactionary, one gathered, though also a humorist. Such general information as I have about him comes from a memoir by Alistair Cooke, called *Six Men*. HL Mencken was a German- American who lived in Baltimore, born in 1880. Cooke met him for the last time in 1955. There was a reference in their conversation to Edgar Lee Masters, author of *The Spoon River Anthology*. "I believe he died the same year I did," Mencken remarked. That would have been 1948, the year he suffered a stroke that left him unable to write.

Why, though, would I - still something of a socialist - feel drawn to such a writer - already half-forgotten as well as being in all probability extremely unpleasant? Well, there was a time when I would have said that the very idea of a humorous reactionary must be a contradiction in terms. You can, however, grow tired of left-wing wits and intellectuals, if you live long enough. How can they be so sure they're right? They were surely wrong about Communism (Bertrand Russell being an exception), which collapsed because it was no longer possible to deny that it hadn't worked. So isn't it worth seeing what the writers who have been critical of progressive ideas all along have been saying? PJ O'Rourke in the recent times, perhaps? Or, a generation earlier, William F Buckley? Or Malcolm Muggeridge, for that matter? Or earlier still, HL Mencken himself?

I imagine Mencken's *Prejudices* were originally magazine pieces, probably published in the *American Mercury* which he founded with the celebrated theatre critic George Jean Nathan. In a world obsessed with political balance, I find the idea refreshing. And my impression from the scanty material I have to hand is that it was his only method. Criticism - writing of any kind - was for him a blood sport, it seems. Not that he was ever given to ignorant ranting. He was a man of extraordinary erudition, over a great range of subjects, besides being an expert on the American language, as he preferred to call it. No one has used that language to more deadly effect.

*

Selected Prejudices: Second Series was published in 1927. This was two years before the Wall Street Crash, which for reasons that will be seen was significant. But Mencken was concerned with more than contemporary events. Here he is, for instance, on the general subject of martyrs:

To die for an idea is unquestionably noble. But how much nobler it would be if men died for ideas that were true. Searching history, I can find no such case. All the great martyrs died for sheer nonsense.

And on capital punishment and a certain public hangman:

Has any historian ever noticed the salubrious effect on the English character of the frenzy of hanging that went on *in England during the eighteenth century?... What worked the change in him? I believe it was worked by the rope of Jack Ketch.*

And on government and democracy:

All government is in essence a conspiracy against the superior man. But here he is also on earning one's living in America: *The business of getting a living, particularly since the war brought the loot of all Europe to the national strongbox, is enormously easier here than in any other Christian lands. The average of intelligence, of knowledge, of competence, is so low that a man who knows his trade, has read fifty good books, and practices the common decencies stands out as brilliantly as a wart on a bald head.*

Well, it isn't hard to imagine how opinions of that kind must have sounded with the coming of the Great Depression, hard on the heels of the Wall Street Crash. And Mencken's reputation was never to recover. But he continued to sound off anyway. He loathed Roosevelt and the New Deal, and lost friends and allies when he suggested that Hitler and the Nazis were no worse. After World War 1 he had protested, with justification, at the vicious propaganda levelled at the German nation, which had fought heroically on several fronts and would have been more than a military match for America acting alone. But with the arrival of the Second World War he had no supporters left when he continued to assert that the Nazi regime had its points.

Even so, HL Mencken can still be refreshing to read, half a century or more after his death. My favourite piece from his book of *Prejudices* is called "Funeral March". It's on the subject of dead gods:

When Jupiter was king of the gods, he writes, *any man who doubted his puissance was ipso facto an ignoramus. But where in all the world is there a man who worships Jupiter today?* And it's the same with countless other important deities of old. He lists dozens of them, from conventional sources. *Men laboured for generations to build vast temples to them - temples with stones as large as motor lorries. Interpreting their whims occupied thousands of priests and wizards. To doubt them was to die, usually at the stake. All were theoretically omnipotent, omniscient and immortal.*

14
THURBER v WODEHOUSE

When I first started to read seriously there were two pre-eminent literary humorists who appeared to be of roughly equal stature: James Thurber and PG Wodehouse. The one who caught my interest at the time was Thurber. I scarcely glanced at Wodehouse, for I had picked up that he was the author of lots of silly comic novels about soppy, well-to-do young men and their equally soppy girlfriends, who were forever trying to snare them into marriage. It seemed so far from the real world I knew - not to mention my socialist beliefs - that I wasn't prepared to give his books the smallest attention. I didn't realise the appeal was chiefly in the choice and arrangement of words on the page, rather than the content. It was a long time as well before I even learnt how to pronounce Wodehouse's name correctly (something that Jack Trevor Story never did manage).

But Thurber I took to instantly, the fact that he was a cartoonist as well as a writer probably helping. Also the fact that he was American, for my literary antennae were leading me strongly in that direction. But then no sooner had I started reading him than he was *dead*. It was my first bereavement of that kind.

I heard about it in unusual circumstances, too. This was in the days of National Service, which I was dodging by working as an engineer in the Merchant Navy, an exempt occupation. It wasn't for long because, as everyone knew, National Service would soon be coming to an end, but I did get through a lot of books - books I'd picked from Percival's while on leave between trips. In fact the circumstances on board ship were even better for reading than having a daily train journey. It's true that we had plenty of booze, and sleep to sleep afterwards, but the time away at sea could still be difficult to fill unless you were a reader, with only the sea itself to gaze at and reflect upon. When we were crossing the Atlantic I would read for hours on end.

I was also of an age when I found it difficult to resist trying to interest others in the books and writers I was discovering. One day, tied up back in Liverpool after a trip to the West Indies and South America, I showed a fellow engineer an already well-thumbed Thurber paperback, hoping he might ask to borrow it.

The man looked puzzled.

"But he's just *died,*" he said. "Haven't you heard?"

"What? *Who's* died?"

"Him! James What's-his-name... *Thurber,* is it?"

It turned out that the engineer lived near the docks and had been home already and seen it on the television news. He had no idea who James Thurber was, but recognised the name. I was shocked, and felt a fool as well. *I* was the one who was supposed know all about writers like Thurber. That would have been in November 1961, and he was sixty-six when he died, so I suppose it's small wonder that he's a long way down the road to being forgotten now. It was half a century ago.

Yet I still can't believe it. Thurber in danger of being forgotten? But then where are his books: *Let Your Mind Alone!, The Middle-Aged Man on the Flying Trapeze, My World and Welcome to It, Thurber Country, Is Sex* Necessary?, *Fables for Our Time, The Thurber Album, The Beast in Me and Other Animals, The Thurber*

Carnival… to name a few off the top of my head? They used to be available in Penguin, but all I've seen in relatively recent times is a solitary anthology entitled *The Secret Life of Walter Mitty*, which looked to be the old *Thurber Carnival*, with a different name.

*

It's very different with PG Wodehouse. There are whole *shelves* full of his books, in a variety of editions, in the big bookshops. He was older than Thurber, but he lived longer and died more recently (1975). Did that make a difference, or was it something else?

But I don't want to give the impression that I still have an aversion to Wodehouse. It isn't so. Some of the titles I see displayed are by now like old friends, too, for I long ago became a fan - or at any rate a *partial* fan. And I remember the night of my conversion.

I had realised that my father loved the *Jeeves* stories, and so had bought him an omnibus edition as a Christmas present. I'm not sure whose idea it was, but I eventually borrowed it to read myself. It might not have happened, though, had our younger daughter, only three or four at the time, not been taken ill with whooping cough. The situation was in fact so worrying that I sat up with her through all of one night. There was no crisis, however, and I spent most of the night reading Wodehouse. I pretty well finished the whole book at a single sitting, and was captivated. Indeed, by morning I felt fresher than I had before not going to bed!

As I've already said elsewhere, though, anyone inclined to dip into Wodehouse for the first time should *avoid* the *Jeeves* books. They will spoil you for the rest. I know I've struggled myself to get through the *Blandings Castle* novels, and they're reckoned to be the next best thing. The only other Wodehouse title I can remember truly enjoying is a slim collection of non-fiction pieces, *Louder* and *Funnier*. Like Evelyn Waugh's *The Ordeal of Gilber Pinfold*, it also happens to be the one that you can never find. And I don't even have an old paperback. I think I must have borrowed it once from the library - still a rare thing for me - though I doubt if you'd find it there now.

But why, as I say, does PG Wodehouse remain so much in demand, while Thurber is nowadays neglected or forgotten? Is it because Thurber wrote short pieces, rather than novels? Has his humour dated, perhaps? Was there a racist element in his work? Or could his decline in popularity even be due to the quiet work of feminists?

Well, Thurber himself once said that everything he wrote seemed to peter out after a couple of thousand words, which could be interpreted as self-criticism. Truman Capote apparently thought that he had never been very funny, and that was an opinion stated some time ago, so if it was true then it will be even more true now. As for any racist content, it has to be admitted that he was fond of making fun of his black servants, such as Della in "What Do You Mean It Was Brillig?"- a piece included in *The Thurber Carnival,* and also in the two-volume collection edited by his second wife, Helen, and first published two years after his death, *Vintage Thurber*. The more likely reason, though, for his slow, posthumous decline, could be the misogynist element in his work - even if it is of a similar kind to that found in the films of Laurel and Hardy.

There is a story, for instance, called "The Private Life of Mr Bidwell", in which the only domestic entertainment the hero can find for himself (this is long before the days of television) is to hold his breath for as long as possible, though his wife of course soon puts a stop even to that. I've no direct evidence, but maybe that would be too much for the feminists, or even for most women in general. But not for some men, I fancy.

I am reminded of a TV item some time ago, featuring the Laurel & Hardy museum in Ulverston, birthplace of Stan Laurel, on the edge of the Lake District, where there is a little cinema showing their films around the clock. Coaches were arriving and it was the men's first port of call, even before the pub, while their wives preferred to go shopping in the town. Later, one of the wives told the TV interviewer that she found their films "sinister".

You might find some of Thurber's pieces "sinister', too, if you have feminist leanings. But then there is surely that same misogynistic streak in Wodehouse's stories, and it doesn't seem to have done *him* any harm. So I don't know. I can only say that I still find Thurber as funny as ever, and would urge anyone sufficiently interested to hunt in particular for his 1930s book, *Let Your Mind Alone!*, in which he makes hilarious, though seriously devastating fun of the inspirational books of the period - volumes with titles like *Streamline Your Mind, How to* Worry *Successfully* and *Be Glad You're Neurotic*. For more than forty years now its message has been carefully stored away in my mind, ready to protect me from updated versions of the same nonsense. (I'm thinking of the training courses and such which used to be unavoidable, working for a big company. Much of this sort of thing goes on in hotels, and I was surprised some years ago by Alan Bennett, in his TV film "Dinner at Noon". Hanging around a large hotel in Harrogate he encountered just such a business gathering, but he could only sympathise with the poor souls who had had to "go back to school". He missed an opportunity. He should have tried to eavesdrop, or simply barged in and had a look at the flip-charts!)

*

Much of James Thurber's finest work appeared first in the New Yorker, in the days when it was edited by Harold Ross - a time later recaptured by Thurber in *The Years with Ross*. His best known story, and the reason why he'll never be completely forgotten, appeared first in those pages, too: 'The Secret Life of Walter Mitty". Everyone has heard of Walter Mitty types - pathetic, seriously deluded men who are some way past their physical prime.

That seems to be the idea, anyway, though I don't myself believe the "real" Walter Mitty was quite like that. It's true that his fantasies did compensate for the lack of adventure and romance in his own humdrum existence, but he didn't tell a soul about them, nor did he act them out for others to see. It was all a very private matter - a *secret life* - confined to the inside of his own head. And nor was it entirely pathetic, for there were strongly felt imaginary victories to be savoured, where none were available to him in the real world.

If you happen to find an old copy of *Let Your Mind Alone!*, he had already put the same sort of idea into a piece called 'The Case for the Daydreamer". After being refused free entry in humiliating fashion by an official, a Mr Bustard, to a dog show on which he is supposed to be reporting, because he has forgotten his press pass, the narrator, instead of simply paying, wanders the streets tor a while imagining, and quietly savouring, a more successful confrontation:

Bertrand Russell at the Free Trade Hall

…In this fancied encounter I in fact enraged Mr Bustard. He lunged at me, whereupon, side-stepping agilely, I led with my left and floored him with a beautiful right to the jaw. 'Try that one!" I cried. "Mercy me!" murmured an old lady who was passing. I began to walk more rapidly. My heart took a definite lift… After a whole afternoon of this I saw Mr Bustard on the way out of the show. I actually felt sorry about the tossing around I had given him, and gave him a triumphant enigmatic smile.

Attempts to put Walter Mitty - or Thurber himself - on the screen have not been very successful, it seems to me. There was that Danny Kaye film, for example - long ago in the 1940s - which portrayed Mitty in a farcical, slapstick kind of way. But then it would have been difficult to film the story as written. His fantasies weren't necessarily sparked off by things that were happening in his real life. More often they occupied periods of boredom, when he had nothing better to do. Right at the end, for example, he is left waiting while his wife goes into a drugstore to buy something. He stands against a wall, smoking… Then he pulls his shoulders back, and his heels together…

'To hell with the handkerchief!" said Walter Mitty scornfully. He took one last drag on his cigarette and snapped it away. Then, with that faint, fleeting smile playing about his lips, he faced the firing squad…

*

But what of Thurber the cartoonist? The *Times* once described him as "a strangely gifted artist". His drawings are pretty crude, obviously done very rapidly, and yet they are inimitable and convey perfectly the people and situations they represent. That is what is puzzling about them. How is this achieved?

My guess is that the drawing often preceded the caption. I don't mean that the cartoon was done without any idea of what it was meant to suggest, only that the caption wasn't settled on finally until the drawing was complete. Typically, you hove a man and a woman - or sometimes two women - facing one another in simple, shapeless armchairs. In the best example I can think of the man is pointing a finger at his (I presume) wife. He could be saying almost anything - until you look at the woman. Then there can be only one caption:

'That martyred look won't get you anywhere with me!"

I would say that there has been a little too much attention given to his dogs, his weedy men with *pince-nez* perched on their noses, and their domineering wives. The real James Thurber wasn't the mild and gentle man of popular myth, but a tough Midwesterner. I like the illustration on the cover of my ancient copy of *Let Your Mind Alone!* - and this time he is illustrating the text. It has the caption: "Motorman Concealing His Sex Life from a Woman Psychologist". The man has a big moustache, and stubble. He is leaning slightly away from the enquiring woman, but his arms are tightly folded, his legs crossed, and his face set in a determined expression. He isn't going to give an inch.

Another favourite is again to be found in the same volume. It shows a man demonstrating the correct technique for "leading a lady to a table in a restaurant" - just the sort of "problem" thrown up by the inspirationalist authors, which Thurber himself somehow happened never to have been troubled by.

Neither drawing is included in *Vintage Thurber*, which nevertheless contains a feast of his extraordinary draughtsmanship. I first delighted in his cartoons fifty years ago, but many have stayed in my mind. There's a drawing, for example, of an elderly man of an earlier time seated, head bowed, in a baronial hall, with a bystander whispering to his companion: "He's just heard about the changes that are taking place in civilisation." Equally memorable is one with two women sitting across a small coffee table. One looks self-assured, the other worried. The self-assured one is saying: "I wouldn't be uneasy - one of my husbands was gone for three weeks."

But best of all for me is his master class in cartoon form on one of his favourite themes, 'The Masculine Approach". These are illustrations again, although the captions alone are very nearly sufficient: "The Indifference Attitude", 'The I-may be-going-away-for-a-year-or-two Move", 'The Letter- writing Method", "The Candy-and-flowers Campaign", and so on. Perhaps less amusing is a series of drawings with the title 'The War Between Men and Women", which was nevertheless a favourite of Dorothy Parker's. I need hardly add that *Vintage Thurber* also contains pretty well all of his best prose writings and is well worth tracking down.

*

From the early 1940s onward, Thurber's drawings became even cruder. One day my elder daughter, who had seen his books on our shelves at home, commented on the drawings in a paperback of a Thurber fable called *The White Deer* that had turned up at school. I had to explain to her that they had been drawn with the help of special equipment when he was almost blind.

Brian Darwent

Not everyone knows that James Thurber was shot in the eye with an arrow when he was young, while playing Cowboys and Indians (or it could have been William Tell) with one of his brothers. The other eye was also affected, but mercifully he kept his sight in it until it finally deteriorated in middle age - by which time his greatest days on the *New Yorker* were behind him - luckily for us! For the remaining ten years of his life he was blind.

His brother never married.

15
HENRY JAMES: A PERSONAL VIEW

How do we find out about writers - whether past or present? Not wholly from their books, I would suggest. I may make rather a habit of finding ones I can stay with for some time, but even I have often read no more than the odd title before moving on. Sometimes not even that. But they can become lodged somewhere in the back of your mind and if, despite neglecting their books, you think they're important, you can find yourself adding to your knowledge of these writers from the chance snippets you pick up, your opinion of them changing in the process, perhaps radically. In the case of writers of old this process can go on for decades.

One writer who has been in my mind in this way for most of my adult life is Henry James. Every now and again I find out something more, and one morning, a few years ago, I opened the *Guardian Saturday Review* and saw a little piece in their *Writers on Writers* series: "James Thurber on Henry James".

The piece opened with Thurber lamenting James's death, so that at first I thought it must be from an obituary notice - but it was written in 1936, and I somehow knew that James had died twenty years before that. He referred to James's *The Spoils of Poynton*, in which two people apparently give up on love for a principle, reflecting on how unhappy James would be with the the sexual mores of his - Thurber's - time, when the man didn't bother to take off his hat or the woman her overcoat.

It happened that James Thurber had first brought the name Henry James to my attention. Below the title of one of his

121

humorous pieces were the words: "With quite the humblest of bows to the master, Henry James". Prompted only by that, I had bought and read *Washington Square*. This would have been in the late '60s, so I can remember nothing about the book - except that James's long, convoluted sentences made it a pretty difficult read. I gave up on him at that point, though I had a conscience about it - until years later I read a comment by Mark Twain, to the effect that if you once put down a Henry James novel you could never pick it up again. I felt better after that.

Yet in my lifetime Henry James has gone from strength to strength. He seemed somewhat forgotten forty years ago, but most people today who read at all seriously will have heard of him, and maybe even have read one of his books. How has this happened? Are modern readers made of stronger stuff than me? Well, it may have something to do with the several wonderful films that have been made of his novels in more recent times - *The Golden Bowl*, to mention one. EM Forster has found new readers in this way, too. (And I do enjoy the films.)

The best film for me of a novel by a writer of the same period as Henry James, though, is Edith Wharton's *House of Mirth*, and I have also listened to an account on the radio of a motor-car journey they made through France when such travel was new and difficult. That changed my opinion of the man again. I began to see him as a creature of flesh and blood, rather than the artist who observed life from a window we hear about. It matched more closely the odd portrait, or photograph, I've come across showing a swarthy, masculine sort of fellow. One such portrait accompanied the short piece by Thurber in the *Guardian*.

*

But that isn't all I have to say. My view of Henry James will for ever be dominated by certain things Somerset Maugham wrote about him. Towards the end of his life Maugham was much the more famous, but now the situation has changed. Few people read him any more, in part perhaps because his novels haven't lent themselves quite so well to the "Merchant-Ivory" treatment. I don't believe Maugham was writing with any malice, though, for the collection of essays - *The Vagrant* Mood - in which his remarks appear belongs to that late period.

Maugham was old enough to have *known* Henry James, and so had a more direct - in fact a personal - view of the man, which always makes a difference. He recalls the occasion when he attended the opening night of James's first play, *Guy Domville*. It was a spectacular disaster, it seems. "One blushed for the author," Maugham writes. Poor James mounted the stage to defend his work, only to be greeted with loud boos and catcalls. He later claimed that his piece had been over the heads of the vulgar public, but in Maugham's opinion it was simply a very bad play. 'The conduct and motives of his characters were not, as in so much of his work, those of normal human beings."

This was in the period of Maugham's own early stage success, and on another occasion James wanted to ask his opinion of an actress who had appeared in one of *his* plays. But he could never be direct. He led up to his enquiry "like a big-game hunter stalking an antelope", groping as ever for the right word - until at last somebody helped him out by asking bluntly, "Do you mean is she a *lady?*" He hated others supplying the right word for him.

Another friend of Maugham's once attempted to help in a similar situation by saying, "Oh, Mr James, I'm not of any importance. *Any* old word is good enough for me" - and deeply offended him.

"No one who knew Henry James in the flesh can read his stories dispassionately," Maugham states. "He got the sound of his voice into every line he wrote."

More damning, though, were his social attitudes. "It seemed to him more than a little ridiculous that, outside of the arts, anyone should be under the necessity of earning a living. The death of a member of the lower orders could be trusted to elicit from him a mild chuckle."

16
MY LIFE WITH JK GALBRAITH

There are famous people whose death you await with… well, not dread exactly. A kind of resigned patience, perhaps. You simply know that no matter how long they may live, one day for certain you're going to read that they've died. I had that feeling strongly with Bertrand Russell - my great hero in my younger days, of course. It looked as if he might go on for ever - live to be a hundred, anyway. But then one morning in February 1970 the *Guardian* dropped on my doormat, and there suddenly was his picture on the front page, his death the main headline. He'd reached the age of ninety-seven. And a few years ago I read that another old hero whose death I had been awaiting with the same resigned patience had died: the economist JK Galbraith. He'd lived to be ninety-seven, too.

The excellent new Routledge editions of his books mean that Russell remains visibly in print in the big bookshops. Not so Galbraith. Thirty years ago he was more in evidence, with a string of blue Pelican paperbacks prominent on the shelves. They included *The Great Crash,* first published in the early '50s and remembered and quoted ever since in times of stock-market turmoil, following the collapse of the latest speculative bubble, its lessons having to be learnt afresh. (Nor has the financial disaster we're still living through been an exception. *The Great Crash* has appeared in Amazon's list of bestsellers, while the Governor of the Bank of England has given it a strong recommendation. With insanity apparently loose in the financial world, his message is more needed now than ever.)

Galbraith's most famous book, *The Affluent Society* (1958), in which he elegantly drew attention to the unpleasant phenomenon of private affluence amid public squalor, made him a household name. (He was even mentioned in an early episode of *Coronation Street.)* Its sequel, *The New Industrial State* - which explained why, in a world dominated by large corporations able to bend consumer desires to their own purposes, it was nonsense to go on pretending that the consumer was king - added to his fame.

These books *were* bestsellers. Next came a television series on the history and social impact of economic ideas, *The* Age of *Uncertainty*. That was in the 1970s, but as recently as 1992 he published an influential book on the growing political dominance and strong aversion to taxes of the comfortably-off middle classes, *The Culture* of *Contentment*. Yet his name probably means little to those who have grown up under Thatcher and Reagan, or more recently Blair. Even the *Guardian* made less of a fuss over Galbraith's death than I anticipated.

Along with fellow Keynesians, he lost the argument, I suppose. *The Culture of Contentment* was really a depressing book. In a democracy it was perfectly legal for the relatively affluent majority to vote for lower taxes without regard to the pressing needs of the poor, he concluded. And in a later book, *The Good Society,* he conceded that, much as one might deplore the fact, people would not easily give up their taste for frivolous consumer goods in favour of a cleaner, healthier and more attractive environment, and extra opportunities for art appreciation.

*

But I became interested in Galbraith and his ideas while the fight with Thatcherism and Reaganomics was still raging. I was travelling daily to my job at ICI in a car club with four other people, all of them senior to me. We used to have the most tremendous rows as we passed through the peaceful Cheshire lanes. Men talk about setting the world to rights, but at that time the future of the country, if not the world, really did seem to be at stake. (It would be much the same right now - except that ICI, once known as the "bell-wether" of the British economy, barely exists any longer. Someone ought to make a television programme about what has happened to it.)

I was usually in a minority of one. With Galbraith as my ally, I argued with passion that Thatcherism was taking us back to the Depression years of the 1930s. Unemployment was already climbing to dangerous levels, with manufacturing industry being severely, and perhaps permanently damaged. My fellow passengers disagreed. The "Winter of Discontent" of 1978/79 was still a vivid memory. Trade union power and all that went with it had finally to be confronted. Lame-duck industries would have to go to the wall if necessary. It's a wonder we didn't come to blows. In fact things got so heated that one morning, when I was driving, I stopped the car and ordered a very senior manager to get out. How I survived that I don't know, though in point of fact no one tried to continue the rows once we'd got to work. Nor did they damage my job position. The managers were in reality a pretty enlightened lot, for which even now, living on a generous ICI pension, I am deeply thankful.

But the fundamental economic dispute was never properly settled. Instead, Mrs Thatcher was saved by the Falklands War. As a victorious war leader she became for a time politically unchallengeable. And so the economic ideas she represented prevailed.

My efforts to influence the great debate were mostly confined to the car club, although I did once write to the Economics Editor of the *Observer*, William Keegan - to surprising effect. Soon after Mrs Thatcher came to power he had commissioned Galbraith and his chief rival Milton Friedman to write articles on Monetarism (the economic doctrine behind Thatcherism). In his piece Galbraith gave the experiment two years at most. Two years had now passed and there was no follow-up article, so I wrote to Keegan, reminding him of Galbraith's words - and a couple of weeks later one duly appeared. In the new piece Galbraith argued that Monetarism could now be pronounced dead.

*

Whether it really was, I can't be sure. Although for a time it seemed to be a tremendously important subject that everybody ought to try to get a handle on, I was in truth never desperately interested in the technicalities of economics. Like Bertrand Russell, JK Galbraith was for me a wonderful *writer* above all else. A joy to read, as they say.

But is it possible for a writer who writes almost exclusively non-fiction to be considered great? Well, Russell did win the Nobel Prize for Literature. Galbraith never won a Nobel Prize, not even in Economics, but his elegant prose was much admired, nevertheless. He could be as witty as Russell, though his wit was more lofty, even arrogant. (He once complained to President Kennedy - who had appointed him Ambassador to India - that the *New York Times* had called him arrogant. To which Kennedy replied that he didn't know why he cared about the *New York Times* particularly, since everyone else said that.) His lofty attitude may have had something to do with his great height, for he was 6'-8" tall. Russell, by contrast, was a small man.

Bertrand Russell at the Free Trade Hall

JK Galbraith did in fact write three novels, even if they weren't much like the novels one usually reads. It would be hard to imagine him writing a sex scene. In all of his writings I can recall only one *risque* passage. He was brought up on a farm in Canada, amongst people of largely Scottish ancestry. In an amusing memoir of those times, *The Scotch*, he describes strolling there with a girlfriend, when they came upon a mare in the act of being "served" by a stallion. The young Galbraith, already well beyond six feet tall, ventured the remark that *he* would like to do that.

"Well, it's your horse!" the girl replied.

17
ISN'T FIFTY YEARS ENOUGH?

What is a writer? I ask myself. Who qualifies? Who *decides?* In a late memoir, *Fates Worse than Death,* Kurt Vonnegut pours scorn on those people who may write a little because they belong to a writing group, or otherwise only dabble at it, yet somehow feel qualified to organise writers' conventions or similar. (I think this sort of thing goes on mainly in America.) He asks how the world would react if persons who happened to have a casual interest in, say, medicine were to decide on a whim to organise a *doctors'* convention for themselves. It probably wouldn't be permitted. Amateur *writers,* though, can simply go ahead.

So, is writing a profession? Few of us would argue if the person who was claiming to be a writer was regularly paid for his work and it was his main employment. That, I should think, is the minimum definition. It isn't enough to point to a certificate on the wall stating that you have passed certain examinations and are therefore fully qualified to sit at a keyboard and make up stories. If you worked primarily for an employer - a television or film company, say, or a newspaper or magazine - you could say you were a professional scriptwriter, or journalist. But a fair number of people would still feel that such writers aren't really *proper* writers, any more than an artist who is paid a salary is a proper *artist.* To be fully recognised as authentic, the writer or artist must be seen to be an independent spirit.

But writers and artists are different, too. Nobody would say that *Van Gogh* wasn't an artist, even though he was supported by his brother, and sold only a single work in his lifetime. He was basically an amateur. It's only in the present day that he's been accepted as an artist, you might think. Yet the evidence suggests that he was recognised as a painter by his contemporaries, weird as his work must have appeared to many. And in his most productive period, towards the end of his short life, painting was certainly *all* he did - working very hard at it as well.

Writers don't seem to be able to get away with that. They have to earn money, or few people will accept that they are writers. And it isn't difficult to spot the reason. Not many people would claim to be able to paint a picture to any sort of standard. Rather more would say they could write a book, however. That's because it doesn't require any immediately obvious skill, and the skill it does require isn't recognised as all that special, anyway. At a pinch, almost anyone could at least give it a go, seems to be the general feeling. We're all said to have *one* book in us.

Which brings us back to those writers' conventions in America, and why it is that people who only dabble at writing nevertheless feel qualified to organise them. Nobody is likely to question what they're doing. They're only pretending to be *writers*, after all - so they're harmless.

This same attitude may explain, too, why it is that we keep seeing that advertisement asking, *Why Not be a Writer?* The writing course must attract a lot of people, because it has been around for a long time, and such advertisements don't come cheap. I wonder, though, if there would be the same response if the question was, *Why Not be an Artist?* Or *Why Not be a Pianist?* Or a *Ballet Dancer?* Or *an Opera Singer?* Yes, wanting to be a writer *is* rather different. It only seems to require a decision. Not a God-given talent.

*

So that brings me to my own situation. At no stage have I been anything like as hard-working as Van Gogh. But I *have* done a lot of writing. And most of what I have written in the past twenty years has been published as well. So my work has had readers. But not many, since I'm talking about publication for the most part in what are known as small-press magazines, and you're expected to subscribe if you want to submit material – which you could say makes it a species of *vanity* publishing, for even a modest payment is rare. On the other hand publication is based on merit, and getting your work into these magazines without any promise of reward is still surprisingly competitive. You have to be pretty good.

Some magazines do also run competitions, so you can earn money that way. Not much, maybe, but some. Does that make you a writer - if you win? But if you're not a subscriber you will be asked to pay an entry fee. That's where the money comes from for the winners and runners-up. So you are not being paid for your work as a professional is paid. I must confess here, too, that I seldom enter these competitions on principle. I don't like the way some of them are judged - marks for characterisation, marks for plot, marks for atmosphere, marks for spelling and punctuation, even sometimes marks for *grammar*. It's like entering an exam, and who wants *that?*

No, I prefer simply to pay my honest subscription fees and submit material I've written just to please myself. I must have published close to a hundred short stories and literary articles in the past couple of decades in that way, in spite of the terrible fierceness of the competition. Not bad, you might say.

Then there's my biography of Jack Trevor Story for me to point to. True, good as I believe it was, I had to pay for publication - though I got the money back, and a little more besides. And the book was also well reviewed here and there. But no, that isn't quite enough to make me a writer. Nor is the fact that *The New Saroyan Reader* was published in the proper way, and I made quite a lot of money, for I was of course only the editor, even if I did contribute a lengthy introduction.

The thing I'm avoiding is that the *real* test of whether you qualify as a writer is what people who have little interest in writing think - friends and family, if you like. And there's no avoiding the unpleasant truth that they will think that if you're making the claim you ought to be earning pots of money as a writer. What else counts? You've been writing for *fifty years* now, and no real money to show for it, they will feel - or even *say*. Forget all that rubbish about being creative - you must be mad!

*

But aren't writers and printed words on the way out in any case? Will they survive the allure of gadgets and the internet? Isn't it true that people like to interact, and isn't that the important thing these electronic toys give us. Doesn't everyone have this urge to throw in their two-pennyworth? Who in future will want to sit quietly and read a book - or for that matter to sit and *write* one, when the feedback, if any, will be months away at least? Don't we *all* want everything to be instantaneous now? Who will want to hang onto books for fifty years, as I have done? To handle them, remembering how they came into our possession? To open them and read a favourite chapter here and there, or just a favourite page or a few lines? To simply cherish them? It doesn't sound very probable.

And yet people are acquisitive as well as having a need for instant gratification. They sometimes want to be able to say, *this is mine*. And they need their quiet moments, too. All the hustle and bustle of the world can suddenly become too much. Think of the fisherman. I don't mean the one fishing for shark in a high-powered boat, but the kind who likes to sit alone with his quiet thoughts on the riverbank, not much caring if he catches anything or nothing.

In the introduction to a late collection of his (early) short stories, Kurt Vonnegut describes what happened to him physically when he picked up and read a story in a magazine (it could have been a novel) as a young teenager during the Depression:

While I'm reading, my pulse and breathing slow down. My high-school troubles drop away. I am in a pleasant state somewhere between sleep and restfulness.

Elsewhere, he labels this process "occidental meditation". It sounds a lot like what happens to the fisherman to me. And it sounds like something valuable to human beings that they ought not to throw away by handing over their lives (and their souls) to electronic gadgets.

These thoughts are also prompted by something else Vonnegut said, in a little book called *Like Shaking Hands with* God. (See epigraph.) It's about involving yourself in creative activity - not with the idea of one day making money, or in the hope of becoming famous - but to *make your soul grow*. When I first read that, all became clear. It's what I've been doing myself all these years. I haven't been wasting my time after all.

Well, after fifty years - and I'm turning seventy-three as I write - the damned thing must be close to being fully grown by now. Isn't fifty years enough? I'm ready to move on…

But all I can do is sit back and wait and see what happens with *this* book - written, as ever, purely and totally, and I may say *defiantly* - for no other reason than to please myself.

ABOUT THE AUTHOR

Brian Darwent is the author of *Romantic Egotist*, a biography of the writer Jack Trevor Story (of *The Trouble with Harry/ Live Now, Pay Later* fame). It was described by Stephen Fry as "a wonderful book about an extraordinary and deeply unusual writer and man", and by Byron Rogers in the *Guardian* as "a little comic classic". He has also been involved in the compiling and editing of a number of anthologies of William Saroyan's stories, two of them published in America. His own stories and articles are frequently to be found in small-press literary magazines.

Brian Darwent passed away in October 2022, aged 83.

This is his final book and has been prepared with love and admiration by his daughters in his memory.